FROM NOPE TO HOPE

How I Overcame
My Suicidal Thoughts
(and How You Can Too)

Lorraine Reguly, B.A./B.Ed.

Disclaimer and Disclosure:

This book has been researched and written to provide you with the best information, techniques, and advice possible, which has worked for the author and many others facing suicidal thoughts.

The author has had many personal experiences with suicidal thoughts, and once attempted to kill herself. She has received a lot of counselling from various doctors, psychologists, and even a psychiatrist. She has taken medications throughout her life, too.

Although the author is a certified high school teacher and has excellent research skills, she does not possess any qualifications in the medical field, and it is advisable for you to seek professional help—if you need it—when you are ready to do so.

Note that the majority of the names used in this book have been changed to protect the privacy of those people.

Table of Contents

Dedication and a Note from the Author (+ A Personal Poem)... 7

Quotes from People I Know (and Have Helped or Influenced)... 11

Introduction, Book Structure, and Why You Should Listen to Me 13

Chapter 1: Why Do You Want to Kill Yourself? 25

Chapter 2: My Story 31

Chapter 3: Raj's Story.. 67

Chapter 4: Farhan's Story 71

Chapter 5: Helen's Story 83

Chapter 6: Temporary and Long-Term Coping Strategies to Use... 93

Chapter 7: Identify Your Emotions and Release Negativity from Your Life.................................. 107

Chapter 8: Change Your Mindset by Using Positive Affirmations 123

Chapter 9: Use Meditation, the Law of Attraction, and Visualization 139

Chapter 10: Form Healthy Habits One Step at a Time... 157

Chapter 11: Improve Your Self-Image............169

Chapter 12: Alternative Treatments and Counselling 183

Chapter 13: Acceptance, Spirituality, and Your Will to Change 193

Chapter 14: Create Your Path to a Happier Life 209

Chapter 15: Put Your Plan into Action by Setting and Attaining Goals 221

Chapter 16: Assess Your Growth....................233

Chapter 17: Conquer Procrastination 243

Chapter 18: How to Make Your Happiness Last 263

Chapter 19: What to Do If Your Suicidal Thoughts Return 269

Chapter 20: The After-Effects of Suicide: DK's Story..275

Chapter 21: Additional Resources and Available Help..285

Acknowledgments...297

About the Author 301

The Author's Plea 305

Space for Additional Notes...............................307

Dedication and a Note from the Author (+ A Personal Poem)

Most writers dedicate their books to someone who has had an impact on their lives in some way. While many people have influenced me over the years, the person who has had the greatest impact on me in recent months while I wrote this book is YOU.

It's true that I don't know you, but it's YOU who I am going to help. It's YOU and YOUR LIFE that I'm going to change. It's YOU who is important to me.

Our human bond connects us, even if our cultures might separate us. We all have issues. Our problems might be different, but our ensuing feelings are the same.

We all bleed red. We all feel emotions. We all want to be happy. And we all should always be there for each other... regardless of time or distance.

Thank you for allowing me to be there for you.

~ Lorraine Reguly

P.S. This is a poem I wrote that clearly shows I know how you feel. I wrote it when I was only 15 years old.

As I search into her eyes, I see loneliness
and fears.
Her face seems so empty, except for those
few tears.

These tears keep on flowing, more and more
from her eyes;
She makes no sound at all, only distant,
muffled cries.

She wants to express her feelings, on many
a different thing,
But she feels that if she does, only more
loneliness it would bring.

She wishes that she had a friend into whom
she can confide;
An understanding, caring person who would
always be by her side.

But instead, she has no one; no one to turn
to in time of need.
She feels like she is trapped, and would very
much like to be freed.

As I search deeper and deeper, I see more
clearly into her eyes,
Because, now, the tears have stopped, and
no longer are her cries.

They have disappeared, although not
completely, for they continue deep down
inside,

But she now feels strong enough to regain her sense of pride.

But again her feelings weaken her and, again, I see a familiar tear.
She seems so far away from me, but yet, she seems so near.

I extend my hand to comfort her; I know I'm reaching in the right direction;
But all I feel is the flatness of the mirror, because I am staring into my own reflection.

Quotes from People I Know (and Have Helped or Influenced)

"When I think of all the personal issues you have had to overcome in your life, it makes me think I haven't had to overcome much." ~ *Maxwell Ivey Jr*

"Lorraine is a go-getter and a determined woman who has the ability to fight against all the odds. If you find yourself hopeless in life, take inspiration from Lorraine's attitude and life." ~ *Harleena Singh*

"Her story brought me out of depression once and has helped many find meaning in life." ~ *Tobenna Okoye*

"Her story is inspiring to such an extent that one can recover even from a deep depression." ~ *Sumit Sagar*

"Lorraine's struggles and professionalism has always inspired me. She knows how to handle difficult situations and stand as the strongest person to win every challenge." ~ *Gaurav Kumar*

"I have met many women in the virtual world of the Internet. What I love about Lorraine is that she is one of a kind, and a humble character. She is always ready to help others, and she is not afraid to share her life's incidents with them. Not only does she share her problems, but also gives solutions to fix them. I pray that she is always happy and blessed." ~ *Malik Sharheel Tahir*

"When I heard about your story, it made me feel more positive. The thing which I like the most is your persistence to fight the odds. And now you are helping others to overcome their odds, which is good. You have a remarkable leadership quality to make the world a better place." ~ *Jitendra Singh*

"Being a single parent, Lorraine has proved to be a woman of emulation using her challenging circumstances as a pillar to inspire others." ~ *Charles-Power Obuh*

"Lorraine shows that no matter what you've experienced in life you can live your dreams and empower others to use obstacles as stepping stones. I love her blog because she doesn't fear getting raw and real, sharing her trials and tribulations in detail, proving that if you are willing to help, to serve and to love that anything is possible." ~ *Ryan Biddulph*

"Lorraine Reguly's life journey is a lesson for most of us who think we could not get out of the challenges we are in." ~ *K.S. Rehan*

"My mother's story is one of adversity and triumph. What she is able to communicate is real for anyone looking for change in their lives." ~ *Julian Reguly*

Introduction, Book Structure, and Why You Should Listen to Me

Introduction

Hi. My name is Lorraine, and I've been where you are. I've felt your hopelessness and despair.

You don't know what to do. You don't know who to turn to. You are at your wits' end.

These feelings are horrible. They consume you. They take over your thoughts and influence your actions.

You feel like you have no control. You feel like there's no hope. You think the only solution is to end it all, eliminating all your problems *forever*.

I get it. I know exactly how you feel… and it's awful to feel this way! I felt this way for years. Yes, *years*. I even tried to kill myself once.

The good news is that I survived. I've since learned different coping strategies and ways to handle my problems.

Even more good news is this: You, too, have the ability within yourself to change yourself and your situation!

I am not a magician, and the answers I have for you will sometimes require you to put forth some effort, but if you trust me and listen to me, I can assure you that your suicidal thoughts will dissipate, your mindset will change, your outlook will be healthier, your future will be brighter, and you will be happier.

During this process, I will be there for you. I will help you through it all.

I will help you to discover new ways of coping with your problems. I will teach you techniques you can use in your daily life to improve it. I will share strategies you can employ to make yourself feel better. Not only will I offer you hope, but I will outline the steps you can take in order to become happier, healthier, and more successful in life!

I'm also going to share some of my personal experiences with you throughout this book.

You might not have the exact same problems as I did (and still have, on occasion), but you will be able to compare your life against mine.

You WILL be able to change your thoughts. You WILL be able to improve your situation. You WILL become happier with your life.

The Structure of this Book

Throughout this book, I am going to be sharing some of my personal experiences with you.

I'm also going to give you specific tasks to do. These are the actions you will need to perform to see the results you want. They are found at the end of each chapter and are called "Thought and Action Exercises."

They are not hard. Most of them don't take a lot of time either. They are designed to be extremely useful to you, too. Keep an open mind and give them a try, when you are instructed to.

You have NOTHING to lose, and EVERYTHING to gain. I promise you, if you listen to me, it will be worth it!

Why You Should Listen to Me

I am honest. I am educated.

I have endured a lot of pain during my life.

I have faced many obstacles.

I was raped. I quit school four times. I got involved with prostitution. I became a single mother at the age of 18. I raised my son by myself. I became addicted to drugs. I also had a gambling addiction. I know what it's like to have no motivation or desire to live.

I have suffered from depression and an extremely negative self-image. I have been overweight my whole life.

I also lost contact with my son for three years. (Fortunately, we reunited!)

Despite all these obstacles, I was still able to overcome them and move on.

Why? I sought counselling. I learned how to cope with all my problems. *I found hope.*

Fortunately for me, I have an above-average IQ, and I'm highly skilled in many areas. I attended university for 5 years and obtained two degrees. I became a math and English teacher.

I am still a certified teacher, although I quit teaching high school students. I teach others online now.

I started my own freelancing business and became an author. This is my second published book, and I have plans to write more. I also help others become authors!

I am currently living life on my own terms, under my own rules and flexible schedule, and I am happier—and freer—than I have ever been.

I'm not going to lie to you, though. I still have bad days. I still get depressed on occasion.

Like I said, I'm an honest person. I'm human, after all, and life is not always easy, regardless of where you live, what you do, or how much money you have.

In fact, *writing this book was one of the hardest things I have done.*

I'm a perfectionist, and I wanted it to be the best resource in the world for people like you, who are plagued with suicidal thoughts, perhaps suffering from depression, and are basically so unhappy that death seems like the only solution.

I wanted to make sure it helped you in many ways. I wanted it to cover every possible reason for why you would want to end your life, and then offer solutions to you for each of these reasons. But I realized that this would be an impossible task because if you ask 1000 different people you will get 1000 different answers for why they would want to do this. However, the commonality would be that they all simply want to end their pain.

So, instead, what I decided to do is create this book around the strategies that have helped me change my life.

These are the same strategies that others have used to change theirs, to end their pain, and move on.

Not only will I provide you with information, I will also teach you these strategies and guide you so that you can implement them in your life.

Once you start implementing them, you will begin to see results. Your life will become one that is more positive, and hopefully, one that you *want* to live.

Although this book might not be as long as other books out there, it is packed full of useful techniques… and a lot of honesty.

I decided to write this book in 2016. The reason it took me so long to actually finish it and prepare it for YOU is twofold.

First of all, since making the decision to write this book, I have had to face my bad memories again. In my attempts to help you by sharing my experiences, I had to recall things about my past that were painful.

It wasn't easy, and I ended up crying a lot when these memories resurfaced. I also got depressed… again.

What surprised me the most is that a few suicidal thoughts tried to enter my mind… again. But I fought them off and stayed strong!

I hadn't had those types of thoughts for years! I thought I had conquered them forever. I thought I was 100% healed and changed.

As it turns out, we are never fully healed from our emotional wounds or the traumas we've endured.

We simply learn to live with them, to cope with them, and to forget them, if we can. (We usually can't, but we *can* learn how to move on.)

Secondly, when I told my family and friends about my decision to write this book, I faced some negativity from a few family members and one of my former acquaintances. I was told I wasn't qualified to help others. I was told I shouldn't bother. I was told that I would not be able to help anyone.

In fact, I was made to feel worthless... again. So, I decided to abandon this "writing project."

I felt bad, I felt like a failure, and I felt like I was letting others down. Then I became quite miserable... again.

I even announced my decision on Facebook, and I said why I was not going to complete this book. To my surprise, something strange happened. A bunch of people stood up for me. They publicly defended me.

They disagreed with my family members and mentioned how much I had helped them already, as well as how much they wanted to read this book when it was finished.

Some of these people weren't even my friends! They were strangers to me! But they had been following me, my blog posts, my Facebook status updates, and my life, and they knew I had the ability to help others transform their lives. In addition, they encouraged me to continue working on this book!

Their encouragement meant so much to me. They reminded me that I did *not* need medical credentials or medical qualifications to help others. They said my own personal experiences about all the stuff I've been through—and my ability to keep going— was more than enough to "qualify" me.

They also reminded me that my family might not want to see me succeed. I'm not perfect. I have many flaws. I know that. My family members know my flaws, too, because they are the ones who know me the best. But in my opinion, family is who you're supposed to count on to support you and encourage you, right? Right! But in my case, they don't. And when they don't, it hurts.

My family demotivated me. Fortunately, my friends were there for me. So were a few strangers who ended up becoming my online friends. They made me realize that I truly have a gift for helping others and that many people were counting on me to help them… people like YOU.

One time, a total stranger happened to comment on one of my Facebook posts, saying that I "heal people" and that she "found strength" in my words. I then messaged that person privately and asked that person to share a bit more with me, because I am often in awe that others find strength *just from reading something I wrote*!

She ended up saying "… for you to recover from that magnitude of pain, hurt, and despair, then I believe there's no problem too big that I can't cope with, none too big to make me want to take my life."

It always makes me feel good to know that I have helped save someone's life.

I once got an email from a girl who told me how I helped her. Actually, I have received many emails and messages from people who have told me I have helped them.

In fact, one guy named Taylor and I have been emailing each other for a few months. He told me I was an amazing person and that said I saved his life.

It was so nice to hear that I helped him! I've helped many other people, in various ways over the past few years, and helped even more people during the last six months.

Since I started talking more and more about this book on Facebook, I have received many more messages… too many to count!

Hearing from people I've helped means a lot to me. It proves *that I really am making a difference and that I'm improving others' lives!* Knowing that I am actually having a huge impact on others is one of the things that have made me keep working on this book, even when I wanted to quit.

I realized that *you* need me.

Even though I might not know you, I know all about the feelings you're having. Not everyone does. Even the "experts" can't always relate to them! That is why I kept writing this book because not everyone knows what you're going through. **But I do.**

Because I have experienced these types of thoughts and have learned how to overcome them, this qualifies me to help you.

I've learned different coping strategies over the years, and I've put them into practice. I learned some from going to counselling, some from my own research and experience, and some from my friends.

I will share them *all* with you in this book. I will also tell you which ones have worked particularly well for me.

By the end of the book, if you follow all of my suggestions, you will not only be filled with hope but will be well on your way to a happier, healthier, successful life… a life you actually *want* to live!

You *can* do this! You *can* feel better! You have the power within you to change! Trust me.

Now that you know what to expect from me, let's begin the journey of changing YOUR life!

I will be with you all the way!

Chapter 1: Why Do You Want to Kill Yourself?

There are many reasons why people think about suicide or why they want to kill themselves. Most often, it's not just ONE THING that will make you have suicidal thoughts, but a combination of several things.

The most common reasons include:

- Suffering emotional pain as a result of a trauma

- Victimization (including being a victim of physical abuse; a crime; a rape, molestation, or another type of sexual abuse)

- Death (the loss of a pet, a friend, a spouse, or another loved one)

- Addictions (to drugs, alcohol, gambling, etc.)

- Loneliness

- Guilt

- Stress

- Frustration

- Rejection

- Overwhelm

- Failure (failing a test in school, not living up to your own expectations or the expectations of others, etc.)

- Psychological illnesses (such as depression, anxiety, etc.)

- Physical illnesses (such as diseases)

- Weight or self-image issues (including issues defining one's gender or sexual identity)

- Financial distress (being in debt, having a general lack of money, or having too many responsibilities)

I'm sure there are many more reasons not listed here for why some people would consider suicide as the answer to escaping their problems, but these are the most common ones.

Many people suffer from more than just one of these reasons, too. I know I did. In fact, throughout my life, I have actually experienced each of these things. It's sad to say, but it's true.

I've had many suicidal thoughts over the years. I can think of six particular times in my life when I have had them. The first was when I was a teenager, after I was raped. The second was during my third year of university, after I failed a very important math exam. The third was during my final year of teaching. The fourth was after I was in an accident wherein I nearly lost my leg, causing it to become slightly deformed for the rest of my life. The fifth was after my son moved out and disowned me. The sixth was while writing this book. In the next chapter, I will elaborate on these experiences.

After that, I will share a few true stories with you, so you can see how suicidal thoughts affect each of us in different ways. These are true stories from real people I know, written by them (and edited by me).

I will then share with you the strategies you can use in your life. The book will end with a true story written by a guy whose sister actually died as a result of a suicide attempt, and says how it affected him and his family.

Suicide, and suicidal thoughts, are a serious issue, but the good news is that, no matter which of these reasons are causing you to want to kill yourself, there are solutions to each of these reasons! Some of the solutions include learning and applying coping strategies to deal with your problems, changing your mindset and self-image from a negative one to a positive one, improving your health, and getting professional treatment or counselling.

Acceptance also plays an important role, too, as part of the solution, and so does spirituality and a willingness to change.

27

Clearly, you want to change to change your life—somehow, in some way—otherwise you would not be reading this book!

That's a good sign!

> *"We may encounter many defeats but we must not be defeated." ~ Maya Angelou*

It is up to you to decide which of the solutions will work best for you.

Through trial and error, and by trying each method, you will discover which methods are most effective in your own life. However, in order to make lasting changes, you will need to identify your issues or problems.

It is only then that you will have a foundation for taking action.

Because this is such a personal thing, I have included exercises for you to do throughout this book to help you on your path to overcoming your suicidal thoughts.

I truly hope you take the time to read them and DO THEM. They WILL benefit you! Please trust me on this!

Now let your journey to overcoming your suicidal thoughts begin!

THOUGHT and ACTION EXERCISE #1

The first step in overcoming your suicidal thoughts is identifying your problems.

Why do you want to kill yourself?

List as many reasons as you can. (Please do not skip this exercise. At the end of the book, you will return to it, armed with solutions! This is important, because it will help you assess your growth, which is the topic of Chapter 16.)

_____
_____
_____
_____
_____
_____
_____
_____
_____
_____
_____
_____
_____
_____
_____
_____
_____

Chapter 2: My Story

I want to tell you about the time I tried killing myself. I also want to tell you about the 6 different time periods in my life when I had suicidal thoughts.

I'm not sure if you truly want to read my life history, but hearing about some of the things I went through in my life might help you to understand that you're not alone.

It also might help you realize that what you are facing might not be as bad as you might think it is!

I will warn you now that this chapter is somewhat depressing. My life has not always been easy, and I have endured some horrible things.

In Chapter 1, I listed many reasons for why someone might have suicidal thoughts. However, when I was 15 years old and I tried to kill myself, I had only suffered from the first two—emotional pain as a result of trauma, and victimization.

It wasn't until later in my life that the other reasons caused me to have such thoughts.

The 1st Time I Had Suicidal Thoughts + My Suicide Attempt

I was raped when I was a 14-year-old virgin. Because I was raised being taught to save my virginity until I was married, I was devastated.

My entire belief system changed after I was raped. I didn't know what to do or how to act. I tried pretending nothing was wrong. I was crushed beyond belief. I felt like life was not worth living, and I wanted to die.

I didn't tell any anyone about the rape, either. I was ashamed. I was embarrassed. I didn't know who to tell or what to say.

I felt guilty. I felt tarnished. I felt used. I felt both disgusting and disgusted. I also felt worthless.

Even though what happened to me was not my fault, it took many years (and several months of counselling) for me to accept this.

I thought it was my fault, because the night that I was raped, I ran away from home.

I stayed with a friend of a friend. He was 29, and seemed like a nice guy. As it turned out, he wasn't. He forced me into submission, although I fought him every step of the way. He covered my mouth with one of his hands as he disrobed me with the other, using the weight from his torso and legs as leverage. Then he raped me.

Throughout the whole ordeal, I cried. I was not only losing my virginity, but I was being forced into sexual intercourse against my will. I felt physical pain too, and wetness, which I later discovered in the bathroom was blood from having my vagina ripped open.

Throughout most of the rape, I struggled, protested, and cried. I grew tired of fighting him and began praying for the rape to be over. Eventually, it was… physically.

Mentally, I was scarred for life.

I thought I was being punished for running away and causing my parents to worry about me, because I was raised in a semi-religious Catholic family, and I was constantly told, "God is watching you. He's going to punish you if you do something wrong!"

To cope with my devastation, I did a few things. I started smoking marijuana. I also began drowning my sorrows by eating and escaped my feelings by sleeping more. I fell into a deep depression.

I constantly thought about killing myself.

One day, I tried to…

I don't remember why I had them, but I had a prescription for Tylenol 3s that contained 30 milligrams of codeine each. There were 30 of them. (I remember these details because of the number 30.) One night, I decided I was going to take them all, get in bed and read a book (one of my favorite activities), and drift peacefully off to death.

I got a big glass of water and swallowed three or four pills at a time, one mouthful after another, until they were gone. I may have even refilled my glass once or twice; I'm not sure. I'm in my forties now, so some details are hazy.

What I do remember is climbing into bed and nestling myself under the comforter. I got a book, and I began reading. I read for a while... until the lines started to blur together.

Then I panicked.

It was happening.

I was dying, and I couldn't even meet my death the way I wanted to; my eyes wouldn't focus.

Somehow, I thought I'd just fall asleep and never wake up, but that wasn't happening.

Then I started to feel sick to my stomach. I felt like puking. I got out of bed, and began heading toward the bathroom. I was going to be sick, but I couldn't walk.

My balance was off. I stumbled and fell into the wall several times.

My heart was racing. That was not what I planned!

I got angry and worried. I didn't know what to do next. Fortunately, my body decided that for me. I threw up. It was gross.

I was in pain, I couldn't see straight, and I was really sick. I felt like I was being punished all over again.

I don't really remember what happened next, but I know I was sick for a while.

When I finally stopped puking, I went to bed and slept.

Oddly enough, I was fine the next day.

Somehow, my life went on, even though, inside my teenage mind, I was a complete mess. I began skipping school. I would sleep at home during the day, and go out at night, to bars, with my older friends. I looked older than what I was, so I always got in; I never got asked for ID.

I ended up drinking a lot of alcohol and smoking pot as a way to cope with my emotional pain.

I also became promiscuous, going home with guys I met at the bar and having sex with them, thinking they would love me if I did. I slowly learned that I was only being used by these guys, that they didn't love me, and never would. This all added to my depression.

My views about sex became pretty messed up after I was raped. I didn't tell my mom about my rape for years afterward. I wish I had.

Maybe I wouldn't be so screwed up in the head when it comes to sex and love and the difference between the two if I had. Maybe my life would have taken a different turn. However, there is no sense speculating on the coulda-woulda-shoulda. That's not going to get me anywhere.

I lost interest in everything. I didn't go to school. Eventually, I quit high school, and started working.

The jobs I had didn't last very long. I was fired from one, and I quit two others. I kept going back to school when each new semester started, trying to become "normal," and live my life like other teenagers did, but I couldn't function like them no matter how hard I tried. I felt like an outcast.

I tried to do well in school, and attend my classes, but I didn't like doing homework. I would always lose interest and start skipping classes, until I finally stopped going to school altogether.

I quit high school four times, during the ages from 15 to 17.

I basically partied for those two years as a way of escaping my emotional pain. I worked, I drank, I smoked marijuana, and I slept around.

My life had no meaning.

I was going nowhere.

I even got pregnant and had an abortion when I was 16 because I was in no shape to become a parent at that age, especially given my circumstances. Later in life, my mom said it was like living with a zombie for those two years. *That's how messed up I was, and it was all because I was raped and had my world turned upside down.*

When I learned I was pregnant, I told my mom. I also told her I was considering having an abortion.

My mom then told me a story about a lady named Marianne. Marianne had dated one of my uncles, and I loved her dearly. I wanted her to become my aunt, too, but she got pregnant and had an abortion at my uncle's behest.

Ultimately, she married someone else. They wanted kids of their own. However, because of what my uncle forced Marianne to do, she became unable to bear children. My mom explained that was a risk I was going to be taking if I had an abortion.

I didn't care. I never wanted kids anyway. Well, that's not totally true — I wanted twin girls one day. But what were the chances of *that* happening? (My grandfather was a fraternal twin, so I thought it *might* be possible.)

So, I went ahead with the abortion.

The day I had it, I thought it was the happiest day of my life. The guilt came later, and I often wonder if I killed not one but two babies. Now, I'll never know.

Given Marianne's experience, I didn't think I'd ever get pregnant again.

When I was 17, I met a Spanish guy named Victor. We dated and became boyfriend and girlfriend. I loved him, and he said he loved me. Eventually, I got pregnant again.

That time, I decided to keep my half-Spanish baby. Abortion was not an option—all I could think about was Marianne and how unfair it was that she couldn't have a baby, but I could.

I was 18 years old when my son was born. I was a high school dropout, an unwed mother, and I was going to give birth to a mixed-race baby.

But I didn't care, because I felt like I had been forgiven! I believed that I was being given a second chance—a chance that Marianne never got.

My parents, however, told me that I could not live with them. I had a younger brother and sister, and they were both in school. I understood that living with them would disrupt the family, because babies are known to cry a lot, especially in the middle of the night when everyone was sleeping.

So, I started saving money and began buying things for an apartment.

Before my son was born, I moved out. I found a two-bedroom apartment for rent in the building across the street from where my family lived. I was still close to home and close to the people I loved.

Having my son, Julian, changed my life. I became a responsible human being. I was needed by this tiny baby, and I loved him so much that I wanted to do anything and everything for him. He made me grow up fast, and he made me want to give him a better life.

I knew that the only way I could provide that for him was if I got educated and got a good job. So I returned to school. Fortunately, there was a special program for single mothers offered at the Adult Education Centre in the city where I lived. I enrolled in it, and went every day.

At that point, I was in school because I *wanted* to be there, not because I *had* to be there. That made a big difference, and I excelled in my courses. It took me four years to complete my remaining high school credits. I didn't care, though, because my life *finally* had meaning.

I became very close with one of my teachers. She became my mentor.

We talked at length about many different things. One day, she asked me if I had been raped. I was shocked at her question. How did she know? I didn't tell anyone about that experience!

Intuitively, she knew. She was a counsellor before she became a teacher. She also encouraged me to get professional help, so that I could proper coping strategies to deal with the trauma I endured.

So I did. My counsellor's name was Susanna. Susanna introduced me to *The Courage to Heal* books—a textbook and a workbook. Together, during our sessions, we worked through the chapters of each book. She would assign me "homework" and I would have to complete it before our next session. I still have those books! I have recommended these books to many people over the years, too. They are truly awesome! These books taught me a lot. They helped me to deal with some of my baggage.

Susanna also encouraged me to bring charges against my rapist. I thought it was too late to file charges, but it wasn't.

I debated on whether or not I should. Would it bring me closure? Would *anything* bring me closure? Filing charges was a difficult decision to make, but I DID end up bringing charges against my rapist.

I ended up having to go to court many times, and be present with my rapist in the same room with me. He opted to be tried by judge and jury. He had a woman named Deirdra speak on his behalf. She was my friend once upon a time; she was the one who introduced us.

She also lied under oath. Seeing her lie on the stand was awful. I couldn't believe she betrayed me.

Since I had no witnesses to present, I was found to be less credible than him. Can you believe that? I was outraged! I was a victim when he raped me, and felt victimized again. Even now, the thought of Deirdra's betrayal sickens me.

The jury found my rapist "not guilty."

I was once again crushed.

However, seeing him in the courtroom throughout the process of charging him and bringing him to trial did, at the time, bring me a small sense of comfort, because it was evident that he was scared, worried that he was going to be found guilty of the crime he committed.

I should actually say "crimes," since I was not his only victim. I found this out by talking to others on our city's chat line a year later. I don't know how many others brought charges against him, or even if they did, since I was not about to follow his life or his possible fate. I simply tried putting him out of my mind each time I thought about him.

I know now that he is online, too, and has social media accounts on Facebook, Twitter, Google+, and LinkedIn. I have blocked him on Facebook and hate him for what he did to me.

Hate is a strong word, and I don't use it lightly. I actually don't hate anyone except for him. I will hate him forever for what he did to me and how he caused my life to change.

After the whole court case was done with, I continued my counselling sessions with Susanna… until one day, I didn't need them anymore.

That was a happy day! I had learned how to cope with my rape.

But I kept *The Courage to Heal Textbook* and *The Courage to Heal Workbook* on hand, in case I ever needed them again.

I was grateful to my mentor for encouraging me to seek counselling. It helped a lot—more than I could ever imagine it would! My mentor also encouraged me to help other students at the Adult Education Centre, because I was so smart and so good at helping others. So I did.

During these years, I helped many students. I tutored them in various subjects, and I discovered that I loved helping them. I also did some volunteer work with the Thunder Bay Literacy Group and tutored a guy who had a speech impediment.

One day, while I was doing my homework, a thought hit me—I should become a teacher!

Until that point, I had no idea what I was going to do with my life. But the more I thought about, the more it made sense. I was good at teaching others, and I was good at communicating my knowledge in a way that was easily understood.

As I completed more and more credits towards my high school diploma, the teachers at the Adult Education Centre helped prepare me for university. I applied to Lakehead University and was accepted into the program of my choice.

I ultimately graduated from the Adult Education Centre with honors. I received a medal, some certificates, and many scholarships and awards. I was proud of myself and my accomplishments.

Finally, my life was on track! It had meaning. I had plans for the future. Life was good!

I started university the same year my son started kindergarten. My plan was to become a high school Mathematics and English teacher. (I had to choose two subjects to teach. Those were the rules of my program.) I have always loved these two subjects, and excelled in each of them. It just made sense to do this.

So I worked toward achieving that goal.

The 2nd Time I Had Suicidal Thoughts

During my first year of university, I failed a math exam. I got 48% on it. I couldn't believe it. It was the first test I had ever failed in my entire life!

This exam counted for 40% of my final mark. Because I needed an overall grade of 60% to pass this course and advance to the next year, I approached the professor during her office hours one day. I expressed my plight to her, and she decided to re-evaluate my exam.

We went over my exam together. I explained what I did in each question, and she ended up giving me four extra marks, giving me 52% on my exam. When she changed the number in her computer, the overall resulting grade was 56%, which she rounded up to 60%. Because I took the initiative to contact her and explain my situation to her, I passed the course!

However, during my third year of university, I failed another math exam. Immediately after writing that exam, I knew I failed it. It was so hard. I also knew that there would be no second chance for me; the exam counted as 70% of my final mark, and I was *already* failing that course. But I had missed the deadline for dropping that course (by two days!), and so I was stuck with it, regardless of the fact that I could have taken another—easier—course in its place.

I was once again devastated. My suicidal thoughts returned. I wanted to kill myself. I felt like such a failure.

I began to doubt myself. How was I going to be a math teacher if I couldn't even pass that math class? I felt horrible. I felt worthless… again.

Because that exam counted for a large portion of my overall grade, and because I simply didn't know the material, I ended up failing that course.

The consequence of my failing that course was that I couldn't continue with my final year, as planned.

I had to pass a certain number of math courses before I could advance. That meant going to university for another year, just because I needed to add one more math class to my list of credits. It also meant that I would have more debt and more student loans. At the time, it cost about $17,000 a year to attend university.

I was so disappointed in myself. However, I thought of my son, and I knew there was nothing I could do but accept my situation. I couldn't kill myself and leave him motherless!

So… life went on.

I borrowed more money and went to university for two more years.

Shortly after I began my fourth year of university, I met a guy and we ended up moving in together. He had a son, too, who lived with his mother, who he was unable to see. So, we fought for visitation rights. We won, and his son came to live with us every second weekend. His son got along well with my son. We all lived together until after I graduated university.

After I obtained my two degrees—my B.A. and my B.Ed. (Bachelor of Arts and Bachelor of Education), I found a job immediately. I had to move to a small town to get it, but I didn't mind. I was just happy to have a job in my field! I would be teaching Mathematics, which is what I wanted to do!

Adjusting to living in an unfamiliar town was difficult. I was homesick a lot. I also had to move to this town alone—my boyfriend didn't come with me because he had responsibilities to his own son, so I took my son with me and basically became a single mother again.

My boyfriend and I broke up several months after I moved.

The 3rd Time I Had Suicidal Thoughts

Things fell apart for me after that.

Plus, my son had problems adjusting to a new school and a new town too. He started stealing money out of my purse and lying about it. He would take off with his friends, not telling me where he was. He would come home late. I didn't know how to handle this behavior. He would not listen to me, no matter what I said. Life was hard. To cope, I started gambling a lot, playing bingo. I took cash advances off my credit cards to fund my gambling addiction. Gambling was how I tried to escape my problems.

It didn't work. My problems got worse. I fell into a deep depression. I wanted to kill myself… again. My suicidal thoughts had returned, and I was severely stressed out most of the time.

I was fed up with my life, and with my son. Finally, I asked one of my friends in my hometown for help.

We made an agreement that she would take my son for a year. I would pay her monthly "child support" and my mom would help out with the medical end of things—taking my son to his doctor's appointments, dentist check-ups, and eye-testing appointments. We all signed an agreement, too, making things legal.

I was supposed to find comfort in the fact that my parenting responsibilities were lessened (temporarily), but I soon found myself missing my son tremendously. In addition, the classes I was assigned to teach that year were not ideal.

A teacher's life is difficult to begin with, because they are highly stressed and work long hours for little pay.

Working in a stressful environment with a bunch of rambunctious teenagers is something only a few people can do. That year, I was assigned two math classes to teach in the morning, and an English class to teach in the afternoon.

The 60 teenagers in the morning classes were not your ordinary, everyday teenagers. They had learning disabilities and discipline issues. They rarely listened, and they got frustrated easily.

I did my best to help them, to teach them, to control them, and to be there for them.

It was really hard for me to find ways to keep them calm and controlled. In fact, they were *never* calm and controlled.

As a result, I felt like a failure as a teacher, in addition to feeling like a failure as a parent. My life felt very out of control. I got extremely frustrated. I started having suicidal thoughts *daily*. I was so unhappy with how my life was that I just wanted to end it. I couldn't wait for it to change. I knew it would change the following semester when I was assigned to teach different classes, but that wait seemed an eternity away.

My frustration escalated when I asked my colleagues for help and advice. The other teachers I spoke with were useless. They did not help me at all, other than simply telling me to "hang in there."

I didn't know what to do. I tried everything. I consulted my books on discipline. I tried using different strategies with these teenagers. Nothing worked. I was stuck in a nightmare.

Because I lived only a few minutes away from the high school, I walked home each day for lunch. During my lunch break, I would cry. Some days, I would scream. I would also slam cupboard doors. The noise (and the action) made me feel better.

But my suicidal thoughts persisted.

One morning, halfway through my second class, I nearly lost my mind. I broke down in front of the students. I started crying, and I couldn't stop.

I didn't want to teach anymore. I didn't want to live. I simply wanted my life to end, right then.

I used the intercom to call down to the principal's office. The vice principal immediately rushed to my class. She took over my teaching duties and sent me to the hospital. She insisted I needed medical help.

When I went to the hospital, I spoke with a doctor at length. I was diagnosed with severe depression and I was prescribed anti-depressants. I was also ordered to take a month off work.

Because of that, and because I wanted to quit my job, I had to speak with a teachers' union representative.

I did that the next day. He agreed that I shouldn't be teaching in my current "condition." I also told him that I wanted to move back home, to my hometown. He thought that would be best, too.

As a result of my mental breakdown, and according to the union's rules, I was instructed to seek psychiatric help. So I did. I also moved back to my hometown and returned to prostitution as a way of earning money.

The 4th Time I Had Suicidal Thoughts

They say "Old habits die hard." It's true. I lived this lifestyle for several years.

When my son, then a teenager, found out about it, he hated me for it. But I didn't stop. I didn't want to return to teaching. I did not know what I wanted to do, so I kept doing what I was doing: gambling, earning, spending, and wasting money.

Two years into this lifestyle, I was in an accident in which I nearly lost my right leg. I had two major surgeries to save it. Unfortunately, the accident caused my leg to become slightly deformed. It will remain that way for the rest of my life. I had to learn how to walk again, after the operations.

My self-esteem was already low, and I became depressed again because I was now deformed. I felt ugly.

I started to hate showering because I didn't want to look at my leg as I shaved it. I hated the constant reminder that I was now "different." My self-image plummeted. I just wanted to curl up in bed and hide from the world.

I began starving myself. I thought that if I lost some weight, I would feel better because I would look better. I had been overweight my whole life, and always had issues with my body. Prior to that point, each time I got depressed, I would eat. I would then get more depressed because I was overweight. Then I would eat some more. It was a vicious circle, and I wanted to break it. So, I began to see food as my enemy.

I thought that if I ate, I would stay fat, and if I didn't, I would lose weight. I was also smoking marijuana again, and I used this drug to get my energy.

I ate very little, and I started walking and exercising. I did this for about three months and lost about 80 pounds. I wasn't thin, but I looked damn good. Everybody said so!

One day, I got severely dehydrated. My body and my mind were not working properly together. The various drugs (both prescribed and illegal ones) were having an adverse effect on me.

My suicidal thoughts had returned and were taking over.

I expressed my desire to die to my son. Julian got scared at my irrational behavior and phoned for help. Both the police and an ambulance came.

I was taken to the hospital and admitted into the mental health ward. I was hospitalized for three long weeks. During that time, I was diagnosed as having Bipolar Disorder.

The doctors and psychologists put me on several different medications and observed me while testing the dosages. They also put me on an eating schedule. I was given breakfast, lunch, and supper each day at the same time. That schedule was easy to follow, as the hospital only prepares meals for their patients at specific times each day.

After I was released from the hospital, a bunch of things happened.

First of all, I got mad at my son for phoning the cops on me and kicked him out. He went to live with my grandfather for a while, and then with my uncle and his family. He had to switch schools, too.

Eventually, he moved in with one of his friends, and lived with him for about a year, until they discovered there was black mold in the house. My son then called me and asked to move back in with me, so he could stay healthy. Because breathing in spores from the mold can potentially kill you, I let him move back home.

He went back to school, to yet *another* school, and I continued living my life, doing drugs, earning money through prostitution, and gambling as a way to escape my problems.

Gambling only made things worse, because my addiction to it caused me to lose control of my life. I spent all of my money trying to win it back. I even spent our grocery money and our rent money. We were almost evicted from our apartment for non-payment of rent.

I somehow managed to rectify the problem, but my son got fed up with me and moved out shortly after he turned 19. That time, it was his choice to leave, which crushed me.

The 5th Time I Had Suicidal Thoughts

When my son moved out that time, he also disowned me. He refused to speak to me, to acknowledge that I was his mother, and would not even let me know where he was living. I didn't even know if he remained in our city or moved elsewhere to live!

It was a very difficult time in my life, and my life spiralled downward during the next two years.

Although I hated my life, I became close to one of my neighbours during that time.

I talked to her almost daily, ate many of my meals with her and her husband, and played endless games of Scrabble with her. These interactions helped me cope with my problems.

But I was still prostituting myself, and one of the other prostitutes I knew introduced me to a drug called ready-rock, which was crack cocaine. I started smoking it and quickly became addicted to it because of the euphoric feelings it gave me. Those feelings, however, were temporary, and didn't last very long. That is why crack cocaine is such a highly addictive drug! It's also a drug that will completely destroy your life as well as your mind, because when you get a craving to have it, you will do ANYTHING to get it, and will even consider committing crimes to get money to buy it.

I ended up spending all of my money on this drug. I didn't pay my bills. My TV connection was disconnected as a result. So was my landline phone. Things went from bad to worse.

To top things off, my best friend, who happened to be my neighbour and Scrabble buddy, decided to move back to her hometown with her husband.

I felt abandoned. I was all alone. I felt worthless. I hated my life, and I hated what I had become. 2011 was one of the worst years of my life. I contemplated suicide daily.

But I couldn't bring myself to end it all. I would think of my son and how he would feel if he learned I killed myself, and I just couldn't do it. Even though he was not in my life at that time, I had faith that he would be again, one day.

Because I am a TV addict, I started visiting a different neighbour, just so I could watch TV there. Watching TV helped me forget my problems. It was one of my coping strategies—to do something I enjoyed, something that was fun.

I also started going to my mom's house to watch TV. One night, I ended up staying there. In fact, I started sleeping there more often. Being around a family who loved me helped me feel better about myself.

Slowly, I started weaning myself off the crack. Being around my family and watching TV regularly helped me do this. Plus, in moments of lucidity, I realized how stupid it was to waste my money on such a temporary "fix." After I started to change my mindset, the drug started to have different effects on me, too. It no longer made me feel good. Instead, it stopped affecting me altogether. And when I would do it, I would feel guilty afterward for wasting my money on it.

Eventually, I stopped smoking it completely. I also started staying at my parents' house more often and helping them with their business. Because I was earning money that way, I stopped working on the street.

As a result of the shift in my mindset, I became healthier. I was no longer degrading myself through prostitution, and I was surrounding myself with people who loved me. I was also taking the medication the doctor's prescribed and quit smoking pot too.

My life improved and I stopped having suicidal thoughts!

The BIG Turning Point in My Life

Then one day, out of the blue, I got really sick and nearly died. I threw up for about twelve hours. The next day, my stomach hurt, but I thought it was from puking so much.

By the following morning, I was in excruciating pain. I couldn't get comfortable. I could barely move. It felt like I was dying.

The pain I felt was worse than being raped. It was more painful than my leg surgery. It was worse than losing my son.

I didn't know what was wrong, so I called 911, and was brought to the hospital.

During the ten hours of testing, the three doctors I saw couldn't find anything wrong. Finally, a fourth doctor, a surgeon, was called in.

It was determined that my appendix had burst, and I was rushed into surgery (after being given the option of taking antibiotics and being sent home, which I denied)!

The surgeon warned me she might have to cut me wide open. I instructed her to do whatever she had to do to save my life.

I spent six days in the hospital and had an epiphany while there, after speaking with a 76-year-old lady, who was my hospital mate (my "roomie") for two days.

I didn't want my life to end.

I wanted it to begin!

Most of all, I didn't want to die without saying "goodbye" to my son.

So I hunted him down. I found out where he worked (he was still in the same city), and I wrote him a letter.

He didn't reply.

After a month of waiting, I called him.

That phone call was tough, but it was a start. It lasted forty-two minutes. He wasn't convinced I had changed, but he gave me the benefit of the doubt, and we talked every couple of weeks from then on.

Then we met for dinner. We became closer and closer again.

This re-connection process began in October of 2012. In December, I asked him what he wanted for Christmas.

He told me to take that money and buy myself something I needed. So, even though I bought him several gifts, I also picked one up for myself: a book called *The Writer's*

Market. I had written a book while I was in university and my professor encouraged me to publish it, so I started looking for publishers who might be interested in publishing that book.

The Writer's Market taught me a lot. I learned that there are two options for publishing a book—to get a traditional publisher to do it, or to self-publish. It also taught me the basic benefits of blogging, and how self-published authors can garner an audience through blogging online.

In January 2013, I began a free blog, to get my name out there. I discovered I loved blogging. Some of my early blog posts hit the number one spot on Google Search, too!

I then learned about SEO, and how to be a better blogger. I wrote an e-book, *20 Blog Post Must-Haves*, which I give away for free to my blog subscribers. I also began earning money by doing freelance writing.

In February 2014, Wording Well was born. This is my freelancing writing and editing business.

Although I have not yet decided who is going to publish the book I wrote while in university, in June 2014, I independently published a book of short stories dealing with topics of identity, drugs, abuse, friendship, and death. This book is called *Risky Issues.*

I then started helping others become authors. I added more services to my business. I gained more clients. I made quite a name for myself online!

Now, clients and other people seek me out. Bloggers want to feature me in their posts. I've been interviewed by a lot of people. I've contributed to expert round-ups.

I've also shared my journey online, and I'm now viewed as someone who is inspirational!

I am living proof that you can go through hell several times over and still come out on top!

All it takes is commitment to change, a bit of hard work, and persistence to succeed.

I'd like to add that my son is proud of his mom once again!

The 6ᵗʰ Time I Had Suicidal Thoughts

There are two reasons why I decided to write this book:

1. To help others, and

2. To earn some passive income.

One day, when I was looking at my blog stats, I saw that I had hundreds of people reading the article I wrote about my suicide attempt and the advice that I provided to help them deal with their own suicidal thoughts.

Because that blog post ranked on the first page of Google, I started studying these stats to see if it remained there. It did.

I then realized I could share so much more with these readers, these tortured souls, and help them further.

So I decided to create a win-win situation: I would write a book (this book!) and reveal even more of my life experiences, including the different things I've learned over the years, which helped me cope with my thoughts and also become a more positive person, and I would be paid for my efforts (through book sales). However, I was not prepared for the emotional suffering I was going to endure while writing it, or the negative thoughts and feelings I would have.

While thinking about writing this book, I thought about all the times I had suicidal thoughts.

My bad memories caused me to become depressed again.

After I started writing about my own experiences, I was reminded of the many dark times of my life.

(There is so much more to my life than what I am telling you here!)

Because I shared this plan on social media (and in a few comments and a few blog posts), I started getting messages from some of my friends, followers, and other social connections.

People began asking me for help, telling me their problems, and saying they were depressed and/or were having suicidal thoughts.

I did not realize that helping others would be so emotionally exhausting, either!

To add to my "stress," I was also attempting to lose weight at the same time.

In July 2015, I found out I have Type 2 Diabetes. At that point in time, I weighed 356 pounds. That was the biggest I ever was in my whole life! Being diagnosed as a diabetic caused me to make some more changes in my life, beginning with my eating and exercising habits. I was making good progress and lost a total of 69 pounds in about a year-and-a-half.

But when I began writing this book, and all my negative memories and emotions resurfaced, I started to fall back into my old habits of eating to deal with my negative feelings.

I became irritable, and I started to feel like a failure again.

As I mentioned in the introduction, I got so stressed out that I thought of abandoning this writing project and even announced that decision on Facebook.

Because I am a perfectionist, I always put pressure on myself, especially when it comes to things I write and edit.

I also wanted this to be a super-helpful book, and I felt like I wasn't living up to my own high expectations.

I also realized that I didn't effectively deal with one particular incident that had a huge impact on me and my life, which involved my grandfather molesting me.

So I started dealing with that, and the events that took place afterward.

I am still dealing with these issues.

As a result of these combined things, a few suicidal thoughts crossed my mind.

Fortunately, they were not as severe as the ones I have had in the past.

I have learned to deal with such thoughts when they arise. *I used my own advice and the techniques I learned to help eliminate these thoughts.*

I stopped trying to lose weight and gave myself permission to eat the foods I wanted. I increased my communications with my friends, and strengthened my circle of support.

I found different ways to motivate myself, too. I set deadlines and tried to meet them. I started using my positive affirmations again, and I revised them in certain areas.

I read inspirational stories and motivational quotes. I even decided to include some of the motivational quotes in here for you!

As I made progress with this book, I felt better, because I was moving in the right direction and was slowly attaining my goals.

I'm stronger now. I'm also ready to discuss each of these methods I use to keep my suicidal thoughts at bay and maintain my positive energy and outlook!

Now I want you to learn how to do the same thing!

There is hope for you!

But before I share these methods with you, I want to you read the true stories of three other people and their experiences with their suicidal thoughts and attempts.

THOUGHT and ACTION EXERCISE #2

While reading my story, was there anything you read that you can relate to?

If so, what did you identify with?

Write down your thoughts in the space provided.

_____

_____

_____

_____

_____

_____

_____

_____

_____

_____

_____

_____

_____

_____

_____

_____

_____

_____

_____

_____

_____

_____

_____

_____

_____

_____

_____

_____

Chapter 3: Raj's Story

I was depressed and frustrated, my mind was a total mess. I was crying every minute when I was alone, and put on a fake face in front of friends, pretending that I was normal. I stopped eating food, skipped lectures, and was thinking what to do next. All because of a girl... whom I loved but who didn't love me back.

After losing hope, I tried to commit suicide. At first, I thought to go to the river and jump from the bridge, but I selected a bike crash. One day, in the morning, I revved my bike to its peak and did a sharp corner to skid and get below the vehicle following me. My plan failed and I ended up with some minor injuries and a broken bike.

I felt more frustrated that day and didn't talk to anyone except my best friend.

That night I made up my mind to do something that would definitely kill me.

Being a blogger and tech nerd, I thought I would find some ideas on Google, maybe some case studies of suicides or some ways that would kill an innocent heart. I Googled "I want to kill myself" and I saw a link to an article titled "I Want to Kill Myself—What Should I Do?" and I immediately clicked on it thinking there would be some mind-blowing ideas which would help me to commit suicide.

I went through the whole post. Instead of getting ideas for how to kill myself, I read about the author, Lorraine, and her life story. After reading the whole article, I found hope. It was hard to move on but I thought at once to follow the steps mentioned there.

It definitely helped me. In February 2017, I found Lorraine on Facebook and came to know that she owned that blog which saved my life and I thanked her heartily for saving my life.

A note for young boys—never try to kill yourself because of a girl, even you have die-hard feelings like I had. Before committing suicide or taking any wrong decision, think about that girl, how she will feel after knowing what you did.

If you are feeling anything like depression, or thinking of committing suicide, think a million times about your loved ones! Keep harmful objects away from you! Cry a lot, share your problems with someone, keep yourself busy, and do things you love.

This is what I do now. I take long bike rides to divert my mind. I talk to some special, close friends who I know care for me, and I try to keep myself busy so I don't think about this stuff again.

AUTHOR'S NOTE: Raj used the tips provided in Chapter 5 (Temporary and Long-Term Coping Strategies to Use) to make positive changes to his life. You can use them too!

THOUGHT and ACTION EXERCISE #3

While reading Raj's story, was there anything you read that you can relate to?

If so, what did you identify with?

Write down your thoughts in the space provided.

_____
_____
_____
_____
_____
_____
_____
_____
_____
_____
_____
_____
_____
_____
_____
_____

Chapter 4: Farhan's Story

I was pretty young when I first thought of killing myself. I was 9 or10 years old.

Up to that point, I was a normal, cheerful, playful happy kid. I was the apple of my parents' eyes and the candy to my grandparents. I was the envy of many mothers. I was the perfect little bundle of happiness and joy.

I was good at school and I loved playing football with my friends. But I was also shy kid who was afraid of everyone, especially grownups. Yet I was still sexually molested by an adult male.

He lived near my grandparents' home. This person gained my trust, let me play with him on his Nintendo machine, gave me candies and chocolates and, then, when I thought I trusted him, he took advantage of me.

He sexually assaulted me and then blackmailed me. He also threatened me… and repeated the assault over and over.

For many years afterward, I used to wake up feeling sad, depressed, and tired of living.

I also tried to kill myself too, but I was a kid and had no idea how to kill myself. The only ways to end a life that I knew back then were from the movies that I watched on television.

Once I held a live electric wire in my hand and I lost consciousness for few minutes. It was painful.

On another occasion, I ate some pills that I found at our home. I got sick. I was taken to the hospital, the doctors flushed my stomach, and it took me a few weeks to get well.

My parents didn't know that I wanted to kill myself; I told them I ate the pills just to see how they tasted, and they believed me because I was a curious child and would often poke my nose everywhere.

In my final attempt, I attempted to walk into a running car while returning from school. And I could have died, or at least I should have got injured seriously. But a friend approached me and pushed me away, and I got away with a few not-so-fatal injuries.

I started reading books to escape my feelings. I read hundreds of books in many genres. I loved reading. (I still do.)

I ate, too. A lot. That was another way I coped with things.

As a result, I gained a lot weight.

Most days were filled with depression, and some days were good where I use to be happy and enjoyed life. But mostly I was sad, depressed, and wanted to end my life.

Childhood is a time when most children are the happiest. Parents and everyone around try hard to make the life of their children happy. My parents too wanted me to be like the other children—happy and cheerful. They were disappointed in me. I was not the kid they thought I would be.

I was the trouble in their life.

I not only lost interest in life, I lost interest in school. I did not study well, my grades went down, and my teacher who would earlier tell my parents how wonderful I was at studies now had nothing but complaints of my incomplete homework and blank test papers.

I went into a depression. I was ashamed of myself. I stopped going out with my parents. I took every opportunity to stay alone at home while my parents and siblings went out to have fun.

The only place I felt safe was in my room, alone. And each time I was alone at my house, I would plot my death.

I hit rock bottom, I was depressed, heart-broken, and hopeless. I spent the next two years being depressed and waiting for death. The pain was unbearable.

When I didn't die after repeated attempts, I figured God wanted me to be here, and there's some reason He wants me here.

My family was a little more religious than average Indian Muslims and our mother read to us the stories of Prophets and other great people, including Prophet Isa (Jesus), Musa (Moses), and Prophet Ibrahim (Abraham).

My father would read to us or narrate stories of Great Freedom fighters of India and other countries such as Nelson Mandela, Martin Luther King Jr., Abraham Lincoln, and many others.

One night, as I lay awake, crying at the pain of living, a thought came to my mind.

Of all the Prophets and great people, I have read or heard, each one of them has faced some sort of problem. And most of them had to go through trying times and hardships to reach their goal.

Nelson Mandela was imprisoned for more than 25 years, and Abraham had to leave his family to learn and then preach.

I thought, maybe I am meant to be something more. Something better than what I am now. Maybe I should do something.

Something. Anything.

On the last day of my 10th Grade, we had a party. A farewell party was organized by the juniors for the graduating batch. It was a good day, and the party was wonderful.

At the end of the party, the Master of Ceremonies asked students to come up on the stage and do whatever they wanted to do. Some of the students spoke of the wonderful times they had in school, and a few performed a dance or a song.

And then I heard my name on the speakers, I was called on stage to perform stand-up comedy. I use to do a little comedy and recite funny verses in front of my friends but that was just for my friends.

I had never been on stage!

Somehow, I gathered courage and went on stage and performed.

I did well.

This gave me some motivation, some boost.

I went on to participate in debates and give speeches.

A kid who once was afraid to speak to his parents now spent hours speaking in front of hundreds of people!

All it took was a little push and the shyness vanished!

Then, somehow, I reached the ripe age of 18 and started college.

Life was still very hard for me. I ended up dropping out of college and did odd jobs. I spent the rest of the time alone reading books.

Reading was my best coping mechanism.

Then I had one specific dream.

One night as I lay in my bed, crying and praying to God Almighty to send me death, I began to think about how my life should have been. How it would be if a few incidents had not happened in my life.

I fell asleep and dreamed.

In my dream, I was a successful person who had power and many people depended on me. It was a wonderful dream.

When I woke up in the morning, I no longer felt sad or depressed, and I was no longer tired of life. Instead, I wanted to be that person from my dream.

After spending a long time frowning, I was smiling now. I was not completely a happy or changed person, but it was something. I had a spark of hope in me. And over the next few weeks, I went on daydreaming about how my life must be and I kept on writing it in a diary. I still have that diary.

I found a book called *You Can Win*, written by Shiv Khera. It is a self-help book that has sold millions of copies in at least 50 different languages.

The book contains short stories and easy-to-understand lessons. I read that book cover-to-cover in a single sitting. When I finished it once, I read it again and again. I still read it once in a while. After reading it, I wrote about what I wanted to do.

The change was gradual; slowly I was working towards being a happy person. I made long-term plans and started implementing them. I made a list of goals that I wanted to reach in the next 5 years and I called them the 5-year plan.

A few small goals from my diary are:

1.   Smile

2.   Say "Thank you" often

3.   Respect others and try not to get into fights

4.   Manage anger

5.   Smile more

6.   Meet new people and talk to them

7.   Join a good college

8.   Get along with my teachers and make a good impression

9.   Get on stage and speak

10.   Become a writer

I filled the pages of my diary with such small goals and I tried real hard to complete them.

I wanted to impress myself. I wanted to be the person I always wanted to be.

I ended up going back to college in 2007. I also started teaching Computer Networking while in college, as it was my specialty (totally self-taught), and I went to teach to around 2000 students from different walks of life.

I was in the first year of my graduation when I was invited to teach "Networks" to Engineering graduates and students who were doing their Masters in Science.

I then did my Masters in Computer Apps from 2012-2015.

Throughout the years, I did many things… many good things.

In 2011 I was awarded by the District Chapter of the Red Cross for my work with Blood Donation.

My motivational work with educating rural students was recognized, and I was facilitated in 2012 by the Indian National Congress (State Chapter), the ruling party of India from 2004-2014.

I am still doing good things, even though I am scarred for life.

For years, I did not trust people. I do not have many friends. I am in my late 20s and I still have a hard time trusting people.

But I inspired people and learned to trust some people.

I learned how to set goals and be happy—and I am happier than what I use to be.

I feel more normal now and I no longer want or wish to die; instead, I want to live and change the lives of many more people.

My five-year plan continues every five years. I am currently in the second five-year plan of my life and it is going smoothly. I am also writing… and am even getting paid to write, doing freelance work! I have my own website too!

In addition, I changed my eating habits and started eating healthy. I lost some weight and improved my self-image.

As a result of the things I am now doing, I no longer wake up sad, depressed, and tired. I wake up happy, with a lot of energy.

And you, too, can make positive changes and lead a happy life!

AUTHOR'S NOTE: Farhan used the tips provided in Chapter 9 (Form Healthy Habits) and Chapter 10 (Improve Your

Self-Image) to make positive changes to his life. You can use them too!

THOUGHT and ACTION EXERCISE #4

While reading Farhan's story, was there anything you read that you can relate to?

If so, what did you identify with?

Write down your thoughts in the space provided.

_____

_____

_____

_____

_____

_____

_____

_____

_____

_____

_____

_____

_____

_____

_____

_____

_____

_____

_____

_____

Chapter 5: Helen's Story

I first attempted suicide at the age of fifteen, in 1992.

I was badly bullied at school and saw death as the only way out. However, that was nothing compared to what I was going through at home.

My parents separated when I was seven, and I lived with my mother and her partner until I was fifteen. Then my father's job abroad ended, so I moved in with him. He subjected me to abuse of various kinds.

A couple of months after I moved in with my dad, I took an overdose. I was rushed to the hospital. I ended up being admitted to a local hospital for several months.

My dad started to tell people I was "mentally defective." He also forced me to suffer from an eating disorder, because he wanted me to be "thin."

Looking back on photos and dress sizes (I made most of my own clothes as a hobby), I already was the right weight for my height.

However, my father wanted me to be Size Zero, which was impossible for someone with my bone structure. He would force me to take laxatives and make myself sick, and scream at me to become "thin."

While I was in the hospital, Social Services called a Child Protection Case Conference because I was deemed to be at risk of abuse from my father. The police were involved, but they did not take any action. I was left with my father for the abuse to worsen, which it did.

I was discharged from the hospital and studied for my GCSEs (school exams at sixteen in the UK). I passed what few I took, and looked forward to starting sixth-form College in September 1993. My father had chosen my subjects—I wasn't allowed to make this decision, and had no career plans.

I was living day-to-day, which is what people do when they have severe health problems. I was still suicidal, and the abuse was continuing. My father used to tell me that people were laughing at me because I was "mentally defective" and too "fat." My mother used to tell me that people didn't like me because I wasn't "nice" and that that was why I had been bullied at school.

To worsen things, my mom, dad, and mom's partner started a business together. They bought the lease to the local pub. I was expected to work in the pub for ninety hours per week for £25 per week.

I was also expected to pay my dad rent for my childhood bedroom. He said that if I didn't, he could rent my bedroom out to "pretty, thin students."

My physical and mental health was already bad prior to them getting the pub, but it worsened drastically.

My dad made me do all the accounts for the pub, with no training whatsoever. He told me that if I made a mistake, I would be sent to prison for fraud. (He made me secretary of his limited company without my knowledge or consent, then lied to me about it. He then did not file his annual returns, something he was required to do by law.

A few years later, I got a letter from Companies House threatening me with prison. I didn't go to prison of course, because I had not done anything wrong, but this incident scared me.)

I would take overdoses at the rate of about one a month, as I could see no way out of my situation other than death.

I would then get scared and, in most cases, I would take myself to the hospital, where I would be accused by the medical staff of being "attention-seeking," "time-wasting," "making things up for attention," and "an actress."

I was due to start college classes in September 1993. Instead, I went to the local airport with the hope of running off abroad. I realized that that was futile, and bought some tablets from the airport. I took an overdose, then I worried that I had been watched on CCTV and would get into trouble. I took a taxi to the nearest hospital. I was accused of "time-wasting when there are very sick children here."

In March 1994, I shot myself with my dad's air rifle. I had to go to the hospital to get the pellet removed from me. Another time I took an overdose. I was over sixteen, so I should have been entitled to medical confidentiality. I begged the nurse not to tell my dad that I was in the hospital. Nevertheless, she told him. He stormed into the hospital and battered me.

The abuse at the pub continued for another three years before my father fired me for being too ill to work. I had been incorrectly told that I did not qualify for disability benefits (welfare) because I was working and because I was a student. I looked for another job. My father wrote me a bad reference so I could not get another job.

He also told me that I was too "fat and stupid" to get a job anywhere else.

At the age of eighteen, I was raped. The rapist subsequently humiliated me, and I was laughed at (for real) and ostracized by almost everyone in my local village. My dad threw me out of the house for being a "fat slut." The rapist used to go to my pub and my father used to make me serve him and interact with him, saying "he's not doing anything wrong."

After seven months, I could not take it anymore and attempted suicide again. I was very lucky to regain consciousness. I was in the hospital for a week before I discharged myself and ran off to visit a friend who was at university several hundred miles away.

In 1996, at the age of nineteen, I moved in with my then-boyfriend, Clive (not his real name), after my father beat me in the street. My dad often physically assaulted me. We soon had happy news—I was expecting our daughter, Ruth. However, Clive had the decency to wait until after Ruth was born in 1997 before starting to hit me.

Clive put me through five years of domestic violence. The police and Social Services would not help us. The worst part of the abuse was the financial abuse. Clive would not give me any housekeeping for years at a time, yet he expected me to pay the bills and put food on the table. It wasn't as though we were poor—Clive earned good money but he spent it in the local pubs, most of the time handing money over to my evil father. I was again incorrectly told that I was not entitled to any disability benefits, even though I was far too ill to work and look after myself, let alone look after a young child.

In 1997, when Ruth was a baby, I decided it was for the best if she didn't have a mother, and took another overdose. I nearly died. However, Ruth gave me a reason to live, and the medication I was on for my mental ill health helped me.

Things were sort-of okay for a while, but I soon started drinking to deal with my situation.

In 2002 I could not take the domestic violence anymore, and my health was at an all-time low after I had been diagnosed with alcoholism. I attempted suicide again. I was very lucky to survive and to regain consciousness and phone an ambulance.

I was discharged back into Clive's care two days later, without even any shoes or money to make the journey home from the hospital.

Clive later told me that he had known about the overdose, but that he had left me unconscious to die, or in his words, to "sleep it off." I knew then that there was no escape, either by death or by other means.

However, later in 2002, a miracle occurred. I managed to get a place in a women's refuge for me and Ruth. I soon got my own apartment and looked forward to a life without Clive's abuse. I started college again as a mature student and did my choice of 'A' levels. I was doing well—in fact, I was known as "the clever one" by my classmates.

But then I became involved with a man named Shaun (not his real name), shortly before I left Clive. Shaun was a chronic alcoholic who drank away my money and treated me very badly. I was no longer drinking at this point; I was enrolled at university doing a Neuroscience degree. However, I had to take a year off because Shaun's abuse made me so ill. I still had suicidal thoughts, but thoughts of Ruth prevented me from acting on them. I eventually ended my relationship with Shaun, but he would not go quietly.

He kept stalking me, and he knew where I lived. I was forced to go to the police, who were more sympathetic than they had been when I had been with Clive. However, Shaun's abuse had taken its toll.

On my thirtieth birthday, I was admitted to the hospital because of suicidal thoughts. I was severely depressed.

In 2010, I formally reported my father's crimes against me to the police. They were unable to press charges because all the evidence had been destroyed over the years. My father died in 2013. I got some degree of closure by the fact that he was unable to hurt anyone anymore.

I managed to complete my degree and also complete a Master's Degree. However, I still had the suicidal thoughts, despite the protective factor of Ruth. I would lie in bed, unable to do anything, and think about how it would be for the best for everyone if I died. This went on for years.

In 2014, my antidepressant medication was switched to the drug Citalopram. This drug stopped my suicidal feelings. It also enabled me to get a driving license (it is illegal to hold a driving license in the UK if you are suicidal, and I needed a letter from my doctor proving that I was free from suicidal thoughts) and a job.

Luckily, my current medication has kept my suicidal thoughts at bay. I am now able to move on with my life and look to the future. I have a car, and am looking for work. I am living proof that things do get better, and that suicidal thoughts do not have to kill you.

AUTHOR'S NOTE: Helen used the tips provided in Chapter 13 (Alternative Treatments and Counselling) to make positive changes to her life. You can use them too!

THOUGHT and ACTION EXERCISE #5

While reading Helen's story, was there anything you read that you can relate to?

If so, what did you identify with?

Write down your thoughts in the space provided.

_____
_____
_____
_____
_____
_____
_____
_____
_____
_____
_____
_____
_____
_____
_____
_____
_____
_____
_____
_____

Chapter 6: Temporary and Long-Term Coping Strategies to Use

There are many different coping strategies you can use when you are feeling suicidal.

Some provide temporary fixes, and some can be used long-term.

It's up to you to decide which ones will work best for *you*. Everyone is different, and what works for me might not work as well for you. Experiment with these different strategies and repeat the ones that help you. But try each one at least once!

1: Talk to someone and get counselling.

This is important on so many levels and is my favorite go-to strategy anytime I am sad or depressed.

First of all, talking always helps. It is very therapeutic. Through conversation, you can unburden yourself. You might gain sympathy, be understood, feel not-so-alone, and you can discover many different things about yourself. You will realize others care about you a lot and will miss you if you are gone.

Secondly, most people have an innate desire to want to help others and solve their problems. If you open up to someone through talking, that person will likely want to help you and offer some assistance or guidance to you.

The only thing you need to remember is to be honest about your thoughts and feelings.

The best people to talk to are your close friends, family member, and medical professionals. I highly recommend speaking to a counsellor of some sort—perhaps a psychologist, a psychometrist, or a psychiatrist.

You might need a referral from your family physician to speak to such a person.

Finally, speaking with a medical professional is something you should do because you could have an undiagnosed medical disorder.

Perhaps your suicidal thoughts stem from depression; being bipolar; having an anxiety disorder, mental illness, or some other real problem that can be diagnosed and easily treated with medication.

I was treated with various medications over the years, and they helped me. As you read in Helen's Story, they helped her too. So go for an assessment, some testing, and get medical help!

2: Focus on positive things and use reminders to help you do this.

Think about positive things such as happy moments from your life. If you have trouble remembering some of them, contact someone who knows you well. Ask that person to help you remember the good times.

Also think of some things to do to help you create new, positive, happy memories. Spend some time with children in your family—play with them, read to them, take them to a park, go swimming with them, etc.

Children often remind us that life is for enjoying, not to be taken so seriously! Remember that laughter is the best medicine! Let the children in your life make you laugh and smile.

Other positive things to focus on include your past achievements and your positive qualities.

Make a list of your accomplishments, passions, and the attributes you love most about yourself.

Are you a caring person?

Do you always try to help others?

Do have skills that your friends don't?

Are you compassionate?

What do others say about you?

Write these positive things down on paper, and keep that paper nearby at all times.

When you start to feel negative, you can pull it out and read it, thereby reminding yourself that you're not a bad person, that you have a lot to offer, and that you have had many good times in your life.

If you can focus on the positive things about yourself, you will begin to look at yourself in a more positive way.

You will feel better about yourself as a result!

3: Don't stay alone, get out of the house often, and be social.

Being alone is not always healthy, especially if your thoughts are negative. It's often tough to think of other things when you are trapped in your own mind.

To combat the difficulties you experience when you are alone with your thoughts, it is advisable to go outside, to get out of the house, and to be social.

Even if you simply go for a walk by yourself, you will see other people, breathe fresh air, and open your mind to new, positive thoughts.

By being social, you will be exposed to new conversations, new situations, and more positive actions. This will all help you to forget about your depression and your problems!

As you observe others and interact in society, you will come to realize that your situation is not as bad as you think it is, and your mindset will change.

While these new thoughts might only be temporary, the more you get out and interact with the world, the more you will stop dwelling on your own negative thoughts!

I speak from experience when I give this particular advice, as I have lived alone a few times during my life.

It always helps me to go for a walk, go for coffee with a friend, and see others in society. I am reminded of how blessed I truly am!

You can also volunteer somewhere. By doing volunteer work, you will be giving back to society, you will be helping others, and you will feel good for doing good works. This is another way you can socialize with others, too.

Win-win for everyone!

4: Get a pet.

Get a cat or dog, or some other type of pet that will rely on you. Pets make you feel needed and loved! Animals need you to feed them, spend time with them, play with them, cuddle them, and love them. Studies have also shown that people who have pets for companions live longer and are happier.

I had a dog for many years. My parents have always had cats. Of the two cats they have at the time of this writing, one of them is my "baby."

I visit my parents often just to visit with that cat!

Her name is Midge, and she's adorable!

I love petting her soft fur and listening to her purr! She always makes me feel so calm!

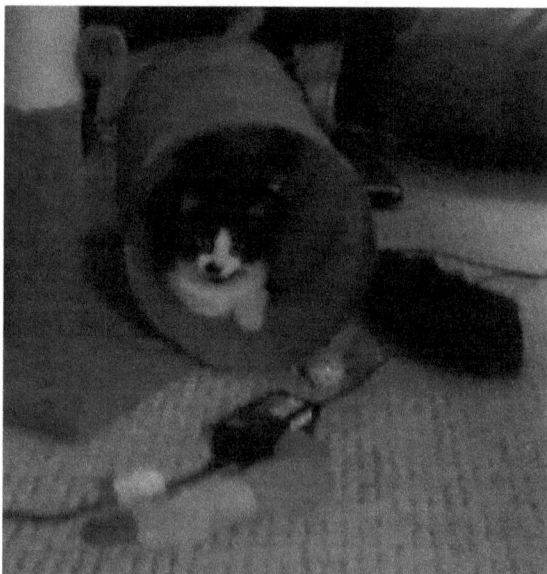

Midge is quite the character. She is very inquisitive. This last picture shows her tilting her head, which she would do whenever she learned something new!

I love her so much and could NEVER consider abandoning her!

I once made a collage of the most of the cats my parents have owned. I actually gave that collage to my dad for Father's Day one year.

I made a collage of my dog, Terri, as well, but for myself. It now hangs on my bedroom wall.

Here are two pictures I included in it:

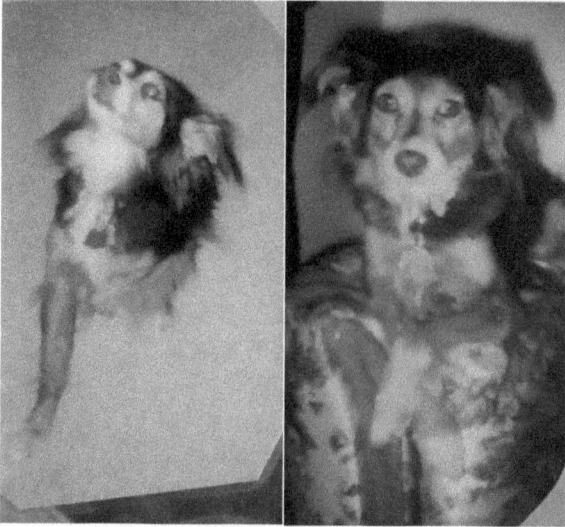

5: Find a hobby and keep yourself busy.

To avoid suicidal thoughts, you need to find a hobby and keep yourself busy. Involve yourself in a physical activity, such as cricket, basketball, baseball, or tennis. Take classes in singing, dancing, or pottery. Start knitting, painting, or writing. If you love cooking, you can take a cooking class.

You can also join a fitness center to keep yourself busy and fit. These actions will not only divert your mind but also will give you a new way to think and start a new life for yourself.

The point is to find something you like to do, want to do, and will enjoy doing. By doing such things, you will start looking forward to your life instead of dreading it! As a result, you will be happier!

6: Challenge your brain and play games.

Games are both enjoyable and challenging. You can use brainstorming games like puzzles, switching boxes, tic-tac-toe, Sudoku, crosswords, and other games to challenge your brain and think of other things.

By playing games and doing such activities, you will make yourself think about something else other than your suicidal thoughts.

There are many free games available online. You can also download your choice of games to your phone and play them at your leisure. Simply do an Internet search for "games and puzzles" and select the ones that you are interested in!

7. Identify and avoid the situations that trigger suicidal thoughts.

Most people encounter situations that will trigger certain thoughts or feelings. It is important to avoid such situations. By identifying the situations or factors that increase your feelings of despair and your thoughts of suicide, you can learn to curb your suicidal thoughts.

For example, going to a bar and drinking with friends may increase your feelings of depression. If this is a trigger for you, avoid going to a bar and stop yourself from being around friends who drink.

Make attempts to notice when your suicidal thoughts are more rampant. Try to pinpoint what made you start having such thoughts.

You will eventually start to notice patterns. These patterns will help you identify and avoid the situations that cause you to have those negative thoughts and you will then be able to stop putting yourself in such situations!

By eliminating the problem, you are finding the solution!

8: Consider how others would feel if you killed yourself.

You are important to *someone*. Everyone is! You have value and worth—you are NOT worthless! You are also loved by those closest to you! For this reason, I want you to consider the following questions:

Who is the person you are closest to? How would he or she feel if you killed yourself?

How would your friends feel? Do you think they would feel guilty for not recognizing you were in trouble? Do you think they would have wanted to stop you? Do you think they would feel a void in their lives?

I can tell you right now that they would feel horrible. They'd feel tremendous amounts of guilt. They would have done anything they could've to stop you. They'd also feel a huge loss.

One of the last chapters of this e-book is DK's true story of what happened to his family when his sister died as result of a suicide attempt. Read it now, or read it later, but know that the after-effects of someone's death—especially a death from suicide—are devastating.

Also, consider these questions: How would you feel if someone you were close to committed suicide? Would you want to put your family and friends through that?

If you're unsure how others would truly feel, ask them. Start a conversation with them. Opening the lines of communication is a step you can take, easily, by asking them this question. Then you will know for sure how they would feel. And you will reconsider killing yourself afterward.

I know you don't want to cause others pain.

You simply want your pain to end.

Finding ways to end your pain is what this book is all about. You *can* put an end to your misery and live a happier life again!

In the next chapter, we are going to discuss ways to identify and release your emotions.

Throughout this book, you will learn other strategies and you can use. These strategies can be used on a long-term basis. Eventually, by using the many techniques mentioned in this book, you will learn to change your thought processes. Your suicidal thoughts will lessen and hopefully disappear completely. Your focus will be on something else (a more positive YOU), and your suicidal thoughts will no longer consume you!

THOUGHT and ACTION EXERCISE #6

In the space provided, answer the following questions:

1: Which of the coping strategies have you already used?

2: Which ones were most effective?

3: Have you spoken to a medical professional yet? If not, call one now and book an appointment. Write your appointment date down. Make sure you go to that appointment too!

_____
_____
_____
_____

Chapter 7: Identify Your Emotions and Release Negativity from Your Life

Are you depressed? Are you angry? Are you frustrated? Do you feel worthless?

When we experience suicidal thoughts, we often feel many different emotions at once.

However, if you can identify which particular emotions you are feeling, it makes it easier to cope with it.

There are many different emotions and many different ways you can cope with them.

In this chapter, I will help you learn to identify your emotions. I will also teach you some ways of releasing your negative emotions.

The exercise afterward will help you to create a plan you can use the next time you experience such emotions.

Once you have identified your emotions, you can implement the appropriate coping strategy for each one and take a specific action to rid yourself of it.

> *"I don't want to be at the mercy of my emotions. I want to use them, to enjoy them, and to dominate them."* ~ *Oscar Wilde,* The Picture of Dorian Gray

Identifying Your Emotions

According to Wikipedia, an emotion can be defined as a "conscious experience characterized by intense mental activity and a high degree of pleasure or displeasure."

Emotions are complex and consist of things we both feel and think. They include our mental reactions towards specific objects or people, accompanied by physiological and behavioral changes in our bodies.

Emotions are strong feelings derived from our different circumstances, moods, and relationships with others.

Emotions involve different components: experience, cognition, and behavior. They also need to be released, especially if they are negative!

According to Robert Plutchik (a professor and a psychologist who taught at the Albert Einstein College of Medicine), there are 8 basic emotions:

1. Anger
2. Fear
3. Sadness
4. Disgust
5. Surprise
6. Anticipation
7. Trust
8. Joy

Robert Plutchik also devised the psycho-evolutionary theory of emotion, which says that all other emotions are derived from the 8 basic emotions and created a "wheel of emotions" to demonstrate this:

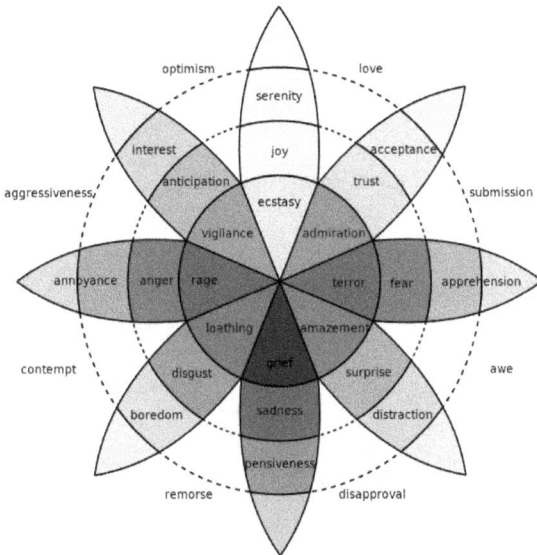

From this wheel, other emotion wheels have been developed.

This next one demonstrates Plutchik's theory in a more detailed way and has been used several times on the internet. I'm unsure who originally created it. The articles that have used it have linked to this URL as the source: http://aca-arizona.org/wp-content/uploads/2013/02/650_Feelings-Wheel-Color.jpg. That site is titled Adult

Children of Alcoholics and Dysfunctional Families. I even reached out to them to find out who the original creator was, because I didn't want to violate any copyright laws, but did not receive a reply. So I have provided all appropriate attribution here so I don't get sued!

Here it is:

Many comprehensive lists of emotions have been created by others and can be easily found on the Internet by doing a simple search. The two I like the best are: 1. The ABC List of Feelings, created by Donna

Harris of www.lifewalk.ca and 2: The Emotions List, created by Byron Katie. You can use these resources to help you identify a wide variety of emotions.

Once you have identified your emotions, you can start ridding yourself of them by using any or all of coping strategies discussed in the next section.

> *"The truth is that we can learn to condition our minds, bodies, and emotions to link pain or pleasure to whatever we choose. By changing what we link pain and pleasure to, we will instantly change our behaviors." ~ Tony Robbins*

> *"Every day we have plenty of opportunities to get angry, stressed or offended. But what you're doing when you indulge these negative emotions is giving something outside yourself power over your happiness. You can choose to not let little things upset you." ~ Joel Osteen*

9 Ways to Release Your Negative Emotions

1: Cry—Cry out loud until you feel better.

2: Scream—Go somewhere where you will be alone. This could be a room, a car, or out in nature somewhere. Scream as loudly as you can. Scream out your feelings. Scream "I hate…" or whatever it is you feel. Do this until you feel better and are calmed.

3: Physically Vent—Punch a pillow. Slam a door. Pound your fists on a table. Repeat this until you no longer feel your frustration. Be sure to release your emotions in a way that is safe. For example, do not hit others or hurt any animals, and do not throw glass items.

When I get angry, I like yelling and slamming doors. I also like throwing things. Of these, the first two are healthy options. Throwing things is not, because it is destructive.

Yelling and slamming doors does not hurt anyone or anything (unless it is a glass door!), and these actions allow me to release my pent-up anger without suffering any consequences. Yet, if I throw something, I might break whatever it is that I am throwing. The consequence of this is that I will later regret it.

The good news is that these two strategies work fast! I usually feel better after only a minute or two!

4: Write—Write out your thoughts and feelings. Don't worry about using proper spelling or grammar. No one is going to read what you wrote except you (unless you decide to give your letter to whomever it is addressed to!). Perhaps you can keep a journal or a diary. You don't have to write in it every day. Use it whenever you feel the need to release yourself. Write about how you feel, what you did, what you want, what you fear—whatever comes to your mind. Write until you have achieved calmness or clarity.

5: Talk—Phone a family member or friend. Text someone. Call a hotline and speak to a stranger. Use social media. Start a conversation on Facebook or Twitter. Reach out to others and share your problems with them.

Most people, when they see someone in distress, will try to help you.

They will offer advice, say kind words to you, and make you feel better.

Even mere acquaintances can help improve your mood. They don't have to be close friends of yours to make you feel better— they can be complete strangers! The key point here is that *talking helps*.

6: Meditate and/or Pray—Use deep breathing exercises to calm your nerves. You can also choose to pray (to your higher power—whoever that is).

Don't just pray for yourself, but pray for others too. Wish them blessings and good fortunes in their lives. This will help release the negativity coursing through your body and open you up to positivity. You can also ask for Divine intervention from the Universe.

Thank and praise the Universe once you receive it. (Meditation will be discussed in-depth in Chapter 9.)

7: Detach Yourself—Imagine someone else is feeling the way you are feeling, and going what you are going through. What would you say to that person? What advice would you give? By detaching yourself from the situation, you can look at it objectively. By thinking of what you would do or say to someone else, you will be able to view the situation differently.

You can then take your own advice to deal with it!

8: Shift Your Perspective—Think about others who are suffering. There are many people in this world who are worse off than you! Many people are homeless, broke, and starving. Others are suffering from terrible diseases such as cancer, which is incurable. Others are in abusive relationships. Others live in parts of the world where they don't have certain freedoms.

Count your blessings, be grateful for what you have, and focus on that instead of on what you don't have.

9: Start Using a Gratitude Journal—This is a practice where, each day, you write down three things you are thankful. Its benefits are tremendous and this practice has been scientifically proven to work.

It can bring you more wealth, improved health, better relationships, and more positivity into your life. Try it. You'll see!

Each day, write down three things you are thankful for. Don't repeat them. Try finding something new each day to appreciate.

You can record them in a journal, a spiral notebook, on your computer in a word program, or you can post them on Facebook.

If you have an iPhone, you can download Benny Hsu's gratitude journal app, Gratitude 365, or any other journal or note-taking app.

When 2017 began, I started writing down what I am thankful for each day on Facebook, using the hashtag

#GratitudeJournalForLorraine.

I've seen others simply use #gratitudejournal in their postings.

You can create your own hashtag, too, like I did. Just replace "Lorraine" with your name!

The rules for keeping a gratitude journal are easy: Just write three new things every day.

After you do this exercise for a while, your brain will start looking for positive things throughout each day. It will look for the positive in your life and not the negative.

As a result, your mind's focus will shift from thinking about what you don't have in your life to the abundance you do have, and you will start to attract more positivity into your life.

> "Gratitude is the healthiest of all human emotions. The more you express gratitude for what you have, the more likely you will have even more to express gratitude for."
> ~ Zig Ziglar

Other Ways to Release Negativity from Your Life

1: Stop interacting with negative people. Negative people are those people who make you feel bad about yourself, who criticize you, and who do not have your best interests at heart.

Avoid such people. This might mean you will have to cut all ties with them, which may be difficult to do if they are your family members or close friends. However, you will be better off without them in your life.

Surround yourself with positive people. Their positive energy will rub off on you.We need the help of others to keep ourselves motivated and inspired.

2: Stop watching the news. News broadcasts are often filled with negative things going on this world. Do not expose yourself to such negativity!

3: Observe your use of technology and social media. For example, when you are on Facebook (if you are), are you exposed to negative images or stories? If you are, limit your use of it. Constant exposure to such things is not healthy.

Also, pay attention to the TV shows and movies you watch. Are they filled with violence? Or are they filled with positive messages? Censor your viewing habits and eliminate shows that do not lift your spirits.

4: Use positive affirmations. (Read Chapter 8 for more information on this topic.)

5: Learn to use meditation, the Law of Attraction, and the visualization technique. (Read Chapter 9 for more information on this topic.)

6. Form healthy habits in your life. (Read Chapter 10 for more on this topic.)

Removing the negative influences from your life is definitely going to help you move your life in the right direction!

You will feel better, calmer, and happier once you have eliminated them!

You will also start reacting to your negative emotions differently, in a more positive manner.

> *"How you react emotionally is a choice in any situation."* ~ Judith Orloff

---

THOUGHT and ACTION EXERCISE #7

Using the emotion wheel, identify some of the negative emotions you have felt in the past few days. Write them in the space provided.

_____
_____
_____
_____
_____
_____
_____
_____
_____
_____
_____
_____
_____

Now, think about how you reacted to each of emotion.

What did you do?
What did you say?
What could you have done differently?

_____
_____
_____
_____
_____
_____
_____
_____
_____
_____
_____
_____
_____
_____
_____
_____
_____

Now, think of some healthier ways you can respond to them the next time you have them.

Review the list of **ways to release your negative emotions** from this chapter.

Beside each emotion on your list, write

down which release method you will use to cope with that particular emotion the next time you experience it.

Having a plan in place will help you!

EMOTION	RELEASE METHOD TO USE

Next, I want you to think of any negative influences you have in your life. What are they?

Write them down in the chart provided.

What can you do to eliminate them? List some ways.

EMOTION	RELEASE METHOD TO USE

LORRAINE REGULY

Chapter 8: Change Your Mindset by Using Positive Affirmations

Our mindset is made up of our thoughts and beliefs. Our mindset is how we view things. It involves our attitudes and a particular way of thinking. Simply put, our mindset is our state of mind.

Each of us has a set of different thoughts that regularly occupy our minds. These thoughts are determined by our experiences, our education, where we live, and how we were raised. Sometimes we have good thoughts. Sometimes they are negative or bad.

Generally speaking, a person leading an average life will have different thoughts than a business owner who is successful, happy, and prospering. Millionaires and successful people or influencers, for example, tend to think differently than the average person.

People who have suicidal thoughts also think differently than the average person.

A very important step in overcoming your suicidal thoughts is to re-frame your thoughts and practice positive self-talk. This usually involves taking the opposite of what you are thinking and reframing it so that it becomes positive. For example, instead of saying "I want to die," you will say "I want to live."

"I want to kill myself" becomes "I don't want to kill myself."

"I just can't handle living anymore" becomes "I am strong and I can handle anything life throws at me!"

"I am worthless" becomes "I am a person of value."

Even if you currently think these positive statements are not true, if you tell yourself something often enough, you will eventually believe it. Why? The human brain can be trained!

Our brains consist of two parts: the conscious and the subconscious. By changing our subconscious thoughts, we can change our negative conscious thoughts and replace them with positive ones. The best way for us to do this is to use positive affirmations and positive self-talk.

Affirmations are positive statements *that are repeated on a daily basis* that alter your current (usually negative) beliefs by sinking into your subconscious.

Even though these statements might not initially be true, the constant repetition of them eventually makes them a reality! This is a strange phenomenon, but it is also a theory that has been proven to work. In a way, it is kind of magical!

How does it work?

If we continually feed our subconscious mind with thoughts and imaginary situations that depict our desired reality, our subconscious starts believing it after some time.

Our subconscious then tries to make these inner scenarios match with our outer reality of life, thus changing our thought processes.

> *"Once you replace negative thoughts with positive ones, you'll start having positive results." ~ Willie Nelson*

How to get started with using positive affirmations:

Make a list of the affirmations you want to use. Print it out, or write it out by hand. Then read each statement from that list out loud every day, preferably every morning immediately after you wake up.

If you incorporate this practice into your routine, and start your day by reading and reciting your positive affirmations, you will begin each day on a positive note.

Within ONE WEEK, you will already notice a difference in your life!

But don't stop there... keep using them, daily, to achieve their maximum effect.

They truly work!

Here is how I use positive affirmations (and my history with them):

I start my day by waking up, going to the bathroom, and then drinking a glass of water and taking my Diabetes medication.

I then make a cup of tea. While the water is boiling, I make my bed. When my tea is ready, I drink it while reading and reciting my list of positive affirmations.

I then review my To-Do list for the day.

I first learned about positive affirmations in 2014. That was the year I started my freelancing business, Wording Well.

It was also the year I first became a published author.

I was initially skeptical when this theory was introduced to me, but I decided to try it, just to see what would happen. I really wanted to succeed in the writing field, and I was willing to do anything and everything I could to ensure my success.

After using positive affirmations for a few months, I saw some extremely positive results. In fact, I wrote an article for the Be a Freelance Writer website, titled "Two Simple Things You Can Do to Kick-start your Writing Success." The first part of the article is devoted to using positive affirmations. I mention some of the sample affirmations I used, as well as all of the positive things that happened in my life as a result of using them.

I am constantly surprised at their powers!

How positive affirmations helped me in other areas of my life:

I have revised my list of affirmations since then. I have added new ones and deleted ones that were no longer applicable to my situation.

I also specifically tailored my affirmations to fit my life.

For example, when I found out I had Diabetes in June 2015, I decided to lose weight. I have been overweight my entire life. I dieted many times, but I always gained the weight back when I stopped dieting.

I knew the only way I would lose weight and keep it off was if I changed my lifestyle and my eating habits. I knew I had to exercise regularly. I knew I had to start eating healthier foods.

And I had to maintain this way of living to see my desired results.

In June 2015, I weighed 356 pounds. This is about 161 kilograms. (Yeah, I know it's A LOT.)

From June 2015 to October 2016, I lost a total of 69 pounds (about 31 kilograms). My weight loss averaged about one pound a week. Some weeks I lost more, some weeks I gained a pound a two back, depending on what I was doing and what I was eating.

I didn't starve myself. I ate regularly. I still ate chocolate and pizza (two of my favorite foods), but I didn't eat them as often. I started walking regularly. Once I was able to move better, I started exercising more, doing dance workouts. I also stopped drinking soda and started drinking water instead.

When I began this weight loss journey, I added some new affirmations to my list.

Those particular affirmations focused on my health and served as a good reminder of why I was doing what I was doing. I have since made sure to use positive affirmations that are relevant to me and my life.

You can do this too.

You can make your own list of affirmations.

You can make them specific to your life, too.

The types of positive affirmations there are:

There are several types of positive affirmations, including general ones (which help everyone), health-related ones (tailored specifically to your situation), work-related ones, and success-related ones.

There are also affirmations for when you are lonely, when you are scared, when you are nervous, when you are angry, when you feel insignificant, when you are conflicted about a decision, when you are around strangers, when you can't sleep, when you are worried, when you can't get your loved ones to support your dreams, and for when you want to give up.

The neat thing about positive affirmations is that you can create affirmations for any situation!

Some examples of general affirmations:

Today is going to be a good day.

I am a wonderful person.

I am confident and strong.

I can do anything I set my mind to.

I am organized and smart.

Doors of opportunity are constantly opened for me.

I expect great things from myself, and I will achieve my goals.

I feel strong, excited, passionate, and powerful!

Today I am concentrating on meeting my goals.

Today I am concentrating on moving my life forward.

I am competent, confident, and calm.

There are NO LIMITS to what I can achieve!

Today, I am optimistic. I remember that my thoughts create my reality. I think positively and surround myself with positive energy!

I am willing to attract all that I desire, beginning here and now.

Today is a wonderful and delightful day—I am alive and moving toward my goals and self-actualization.

All that I desire is coming to me in both expected and unexpected ways, and I am happier with myself for learning how to attract success and be successful in all that I do.

I am loved in many ways by many people and am loving myself more and more with each passing day.

I release the need to judge or criticize myself (or others) and welcome positivity and peace into my world.

I am patient, thoughtful, understanding, and kind.

I am taking the steps needed to move my life forward.

I have access to unlimited assistance and can achieve anything I set my mind to.

I am embarking on this journey to a better self because I want to make positive changes in my life.

I deserve all good things, including happiness and success.

I am motivated.

I am in control of my life and my destiny.

I am becoming the best version of myself that I can be, and no one can stop me.

I am unstoppable!

I love myself and my life.

I am blessed and grateful for all I have.

I act with dignity and self-respect.

I am the only one who can make me happy. I make myself happy by being a good friend to myself.

I treat others with respect and appreciate their individuality, and I make a difference whenever I can.

I am my own best friend.

I am conquering my fears and I am awesome!

I love myself, my body, my looks, and my life.

I am loved unconditionally by many people.

I am amazing and I enjoy life to the fullest!

Here are some examples of work-related affirmations:

Doors of opportunity and abundance open to me NOW!

My financial abundance overflows today!

Success and achievement are natural outcomes for me!

I can do whatever I set my mind to!

I expect GREAT things from myself.

There are no limits to what I can and will achieve today!

I am vacationing every year, without harboring feelings of guilt.

I can have what I want!

I am a millionaire!

I have an unlimited supply of money, and will, for the rest of my life.

Here are some examples of health-related affirmations (some are geared toward those who want to lose weight):

I am receptive to learning how to change my body and life and will make a conscious effort each day to improve myself.

I am making changes to the way I eat.

I am making changes to my thoughts about food. Food exists to sustain me, not to comfort me.

The desire to be a better version of myself and reach my goals is motivating me to make this important lifestyle change.

I am on my way to a healthier and leaner self.

I have softer, moister skin now, because of all the water I drink.

It's never too late to lose the weight that took me years to gain.

I don't need to eat junk food to feel happy or comforted.

Because of the changes I am making, I can move faster and breathe better.

I am making exercise something I enjoy doing.

I am strengthening my willpower.

I am getting healthier with each step I take.

I am quashing my cravings for sweets.

I am seeing results.

I love myself and I love my new focus.

I do not let stress or negativity bother me. I have found ways to curb these negative things, such as eating healthy foods, adding exercise to my daily routine, and remembering to focus on "the big picture."

I don't need chocolate, sweets/treats, or other "junk" foods to feel good or improve my mood on a temporary basis. I am MUCH better off without them.

I am loved in many ways by many people and am loving myself more and more with each passing day because I am worth it and need to be healthy in all ways.

I am embarking on this journey to a better self because:

1. I need to make a change NOW.

2. I want to be healthier.

3. I want to be successful and attain all of my goals.

4. I want to be alive and well when my grandchildren are born/grow up.

5. I will be more successful in other areas of my life if I am healthier and happier.

How to create your own positive affirmations:

When you first start using positive affirmations, it is best to simply use the ones others have created.

You can copy any of the sample statements listed in this chapter to create your own list.

Remember, once you start using positive affirmations on a daily basis, your subconscious mind will begin to change your conscious thoughts.

Your negative thoughts will begin to dissipate.

You will become more positive.

Your life will be better.

As a result, you will have more hope.

THOUGHT and ACTION EXERCISE #8

Fill in the blanks and follow the instructions given.

What is your current positivity level (how positive do you feel today)?

Rate it on a scale from 1 to 10.

My current positivity level is _____.

Now think about the different areas of your life that need improvement.

Create a list of positive affirmations for each of these categories.

You can use the sample affirmations I provided and you can create additional ones.

Be sure to tailor them to your specific situation.

You can also use your current negative thoughts and write positive ones for each of them. Just create positive statements that are opposite of your negative ones.

After you create your list, print it out, or write it out by hand on some paper.

Keep it handy.

Read and recite your affirmations for one week.

At the end of that week, do a self-assessment.

Rate your positivity level on a scale of 1 to 10.

My positivity level after one week is _____.

Repeat this at the end of the second week, too.

My positivity level after two weeks is _____.

You will definitely see a change in your positivity level!

Get started on creating your list of positive affirmations by filling in the blanks on the next page:

Today I am going to concentrate on _____ _____.

I am _____.

I am also _____.

Here is a list of the affirmations I am going to use each day:

_____

_____

_____

_____

_____

_____

_____

_____

_____

_____

_____

_____

_____

_____

_____

_____

_____

_____

_____

_____

_____

_____

Chapter 9: Use Meditation, the Law of Attraction, and Visualization

When you are feeling suicidal, you generally have many thoughts racing through your mind.

To slow down this activity and re-focus your thoughts, you can practice meditation. Meditation will allow you to change your thoughts so that you can put the Law of Attraction into effect in a more positive way.

These two things will also help you employ the visualization technique, which will definitely cause your life to improve!

"It is estimated that the average person has between 12,000 and 70,000 thoughts a day. This is evidence enough to suggest that your goal should not be to control every thought. It is your dominant thoughts and beliefs that you must learn to bring under your conscious control as they are what largely determine your mental attitude. As you do, you will find your random thoughts themselves becoming more positive and more deliberate." ~ *taken from the Internet article titled* "Thought Power—Your Thoughts Create Your Reality" *(found at http://www.mind-your-reality.com/thought_power.html)*

Meditation

Meditation is basically a technique that helps to clear your mind. From my research, meditation actually has a different meaning to each individual.

Some people view it as simply a breathing practice. Some view it as the mental concentration of something. Some view it as a state of thoughtless awareness. And some view it as a way of simply focusing on one particular thing.

To help you form your own view of what meditation is—or can be—I'm going to share a few good examples of what mediation is and how it can help you.

Remember when I said in Chapter 3 that our brains can be trained?

Look at Wikipedia's definition of meditation:

"Meditation is a practice where an individual trains the mind or induces a mode of consciousness… to promote relaxation, build internal energy or life force and develop compassion, love, patience, generosity, and forgiveness."

The website called The Buddhist Centre has this definition of meditation, found at (https://thebuddhistcentre.com/text/what-meditation): "Meditation is a means of transforming the mind… that encourage and develop concentration, clarity, emotional positivity, and a calm seeing of the true nature of things…to cultivate new, more positive ways of being. …Such experiences can have a transformative effect and can lead to a new understanding of life."

I like this definition because it focuses on emotional positivity which can transform your life.

Maxwell Ivey Jr, a blind entrepreneur and author (and a personal friend of mine), is internationally known as The Blind Blogger. He underwent a major transformation in his life when he had gastric bypass surgery and lost over 250 pounds in 4 years.

He subsequently wrote two books. His first one is *Leading You Out of the Darkness into the Light: A Blind Man's Inspirational Guide to Success*, in which he provides 11 steps to success.

His second book is called *It's Not the Cookie, It's the Bag: An Easy-to-Follow Guide for Weight Loss Success*. In this book, there is a chapter titled "Modern Meditation." He has created his own definition of meditation to include taking a regular, everyday activities (such as showering or petting a dog) and making those moments special.

Using the example of petting his dog, Penny, he says:

"For anywhere from five to thirty minutes, I scratch her back, rub her belly, and stroke her fur. I focus on the repetitive motions and the warmth of her body. I think about the pleasure I am bringing her. I slow my thoughts and focus on my breathing. I get a sense of calmness and I relax for a short time."

He goes on to say:

"There are many times in our day we could use to improve our mental health if we just allow ourselves to enjoy the moment."

He also says:

"Meditation allows you to reduce stress, lower blood pressure, increase focus, improve your mood, and encourage you to make better choices."

I completely agree with him!

You can practice different forms of meditation while doing almost any repetitive activity or chore—while doing the dishes, while exercising, while showering, while preparing meals, etc. By shifting your concentration and focusing on what you are doing, you can calm yourself and change your mood. It's easy to become more positive when you are enjoying the moment.

Another famous blogger and author I know, Ryan Biddulph, practices 20 minutes of meditation each day, immediately after he wakes up.

Years ago, Ryan was a broke security guard. He is now the author of over 124 e-books and now travels the world, island-hopping with his wife, Kelli, who used to suffer from depression.

Ryan and Kelli are now living out their dreams on a daily basis! His website is called Blogging from Paradise, and hers is called Life Made to Order.

Kelli is also an author. She has written a series of e-books on The Law of Attraction.

She is an expert on this topic!

Together, they have discovered that using these techniques together has made an incredibly positive impact on their lives.

The Law of Attraction

According to ancient beliefs, the Law of Attraction (LOA) is the basic Law of the Universe. The Law of Attraction states that our predominant thoughts, feelings, and beliefs determine the experiences we attract into our lives, and it uses the power of the mind to translate whatever is in our thoughts to materialize them into a reality.

The LOA is a universal law where the prime belief is that "like attracts like." This is similar to the laws of magnets! Therefore, if you think and believe negative things all the time, your life will be filled negative experiences, and if you think and believe positive things all the time, then your life will be filled with positive experiences.

> *"By thinking of the good things you want to happen as part of a regular routine, you are creating a positive energy."* ~ *Stephen Richards, from his book* Ask and the Universe Will Provide: A Straightforward Guide to Manifesting Your Dreams

Part of the theory of the LOA is that you can use it to attract situations, experiences, and material objects that you want into your life.

The theory is that if we consciously direct our focus on what we want, we will get more of it. The more energy you give to a particular thought, the greater its power.

Because our beliefs determine how we think and how we feel, they also determine our energy—how we move through the world. By changing our thoughts, we change our energy. Our energy is the only thing we really have any control over.

However, there is something important you need to know: The only way to manifest your thoughts into things is to believe and live as if you have already accomplished your goal!

Therefore, changing your current belief system is crucial to using The Law of Attraction successfully.

This is where visualization comes into play.

> *"All that we are is the result of what we have thought. The mind is everything. What we think, we become." ~ Buddha (Siddhartha Gautama)*

Visualization

The visualization technique is used in conjunction with meditation, and also involves The Law of Attraction. By combining these three things, you can basically get what you want out of life!

The practice of visualization is actually quite simple, and follows these steps:

- Find a comfortable place where you can sit or lie down for 20 minutes without being disturbed.

- Breathe in and out slowly and deeply 10 times.

- Allow your mind to picture what you want, whatever that happens to be.

- Imagine that you have already gotten what you want. Let your mind evoke the different images of it.

- In your mind, use your senses to imagine how you will feel, what you would see, what you would touch, and what you would hear.

- Completely build a mental scenario and imagine yourself actually living in that scenario.

- Repeat this process until you get what you want. It may take you many times, but what you want will eventually manifest itself into a reality.

I have used this technique in my life several times. I will share an example with you now.

Let me first tell you about the climate in which I live. In the winter, the temperature drops to minus thirty-five degrees Celsius during the months of January and February. We get a lot of snow, too. During the summer months, it can get as hot as thirty degrees, but most days fall within the range of twenty to twenty-five degrees.

Let me also tell you that I have not done a lot of travelling during my life. However, I always wanted to take my dream vacation. This involved me relaxing on a beach, surrounded by palm trees (which I had never seen before in my life).

On Wednesday, February 17th, 2016, I went to an indoor swimming pool with my young nephew. There was a heated, smaller pool for children next to the big pool. On one of the walls next to this kiddie pool was a painting of a palm tree. My nephew was playing in the big pool with some boys and didn't want me around him, so I decided to relax in the smaller pool.

I lay back, resting my head on one of the smaller floatation mats and stared at that painting, imagining myself living my dream. As I looked at that tree, I imagined it was real. I concentrated on the warmth of the water in the small pool and imaged it was the sun that was warming me. Because it was winter outside—very cold with a lot of snow—that was completely opposite of what my reality was. Yet I continued to imagine myself on a sandy beach, listening to the ocean waters lap against the shore, while I laid under the warm sun.

Four days later, on the night Saturday, Feb. 20th, 2016, I received a message from my brother on Facebook. He informed me that he and his girlfriend were going to Punta Cana for a week. They were leaving on Tuesday, Feb. 23rd, 2016. He invited me to go with them. (For the record, I have never travelled anywhere with my brother before. He has gone on many trips, too!)

Punta Cana is in the Dominican Republic, a primarily Spanish-speaking country. My son

LORRAINE REGULY

is half-Spanish, and I had learned to speak a bit of this language years ago, from my son's father and his Spanish friends.

My brother sent me a link to the resort they were going to stay at and a link to where to buy a ticket. Although I was given only two days' notice of this trip, when I looked at the resort, I was in awe. It looked so beautiful there! Immediately, I wanted to go with them! I wanted to live my dream. I wanted to relax. I wanted the stress to leave my life.

At that point in my life, I had been taking care of my mom for almost three months. She had broken her arm, and I had been preparing all of her meals for her as well as doing all of her chores (which involved cooking, cleaning, grocery shopping for her, doing my parents' laundry, changing the cats' litter box, etc.).

I was tired and worn out, and I really needed a break.

I also had to stop working for a bit. I simply didn't have time to work. Taking care of her was very demanding.

To top things off, my parents had also decided to sell their house, which they lived in for 40+ years. I had a lot on my plate, as I was expected to help them go through their belongings, help them get rid of some of them, help them pack, help find an apartment to move to, help them move, and help them get set up in their new place. But I also had just finished paying off my credit cards, and so I didn't really have the funds to go on a trip.

Now, here's the thing.

I had just gotten my passport in January. I had never travelled anywhere before.

Since getting involved with and using positive affirmations, I started visualizing some of the things I wanted. I saw results, too, and my life had been moving forward for a while.

In the back of my mind, I knew I would eventually take my dream vacation. I just didn't have any solid plans for when that would be… until I received that message from my brother. I took my brother's message as a sign that I was destined to go on the trip.

My brother and his girlfriend have both travelled to other countries before. They were experienced, they had done all the research, and I knew I would be safe with them. They had even checked the weather forecast for Punta Cana for the following week. It was expected to be 28 to 32 degrees Celsius all week long, with no rain. That was perfect weather for relaxing on the beach under the sun!

I decided to throw caution to the wind and use my credit card to charge my trip. Why not? For me, it was an opportunity of a lifetime. So, I did… and I'm so happy I did.

I had two days to prepare for this trip. I bought bug spray (I don't like bugs), three containers of sunscreen (I burn easily), and a visor/cap. I dug out my summer shorts and tops. I packed a few dresses, a dressy pair of sandals, and my flip-flops. I gathered my toiletries, contact lenses, and make-up. I selected a few books to read.

I read reviews about the hotel. I printed off some useful Spanish Travel Phrases. I didn't have time to buy a Spanish/English dictionary, but I had remembered some of the language I previously learned. I had taken a college course in Conversational Spanish, so I was confident that I would know enough to get by and survive for a week without any issues.

I was set.

I left my laptop at home, but I brought my phone charger and smartphone!

We left early Tuesday morning, as planned.

The flight was a direct one and took about 5 hours. I had no problems passing through Customs. None of us did. We stayed at the Blau Natura Park Eco Beach Resort & Spa.

The packages we purchased were all-inclusive, which meant that they included all hotel costs, airfare, taxes (including the tax you have to pay just to leave the Dominican Republic!), all food, all drinks (including alcoholic drinks!), and all other taxes. It was a sweet deal.

I thoroughly enjoyed every moment I spent there. I went from "stressed out" to "peaceful" in seconds.

The moment I saw the beach, all worries left me. I didn't think about problems, work, family, or… anything. Instead, I was "at one" with nature, and extremely happy that, for a full seven days, I would be able to live out my dream vacation!

That experience of mine is proof that visualization truly works.

The positivity of my experience led to many positive after-effects, too, which lasted a long time after I returned home!

Here are the after-effects and benefits I experienced:

1. I became rejuvenated.

2. My attitude changed, for the better. I became positive about everything!

3. I became more productive. I now work smarter, not harder.

4. My sexual drive returned. (For a single gal like me, this is HUGE!)

5. I am meeting new people in different ways now. *Easily.*

6. I'm not afraid of trying new things, or stepping out of my comfort zone. I even went zip-lining when I was there!

7. I created memories that will last me a lifetime. And I took over 1200 pictures to remind myself, lest I should ever forget!

8. I now have a desire to be the best version of myself that I can be. (Even though I've accomplished a lot already, I'm nowhere near reaching my point of self-actualization, but I strongly believe that I will reach that point, someday.)

9. I am more active and am eating better. Ergo, I'm healthier. And happier. Much happier!

Even though I had to charge that trip on my credit card, I knew I would've regretted it forever if I didn't jump at the opportunity to take this vacation.

Visualization is used in conjunction with meditation techniques as well as The Law of Attraction and positive affirmations (discussed in Chapter 3). These techniques work. My positive experiences are proof!

> *"In order to carry a positive action, we must develop a positive vision."* ~ *Dalai Lama*

One more positive affirmation you can add to your list is this one:

I ask for it, visualize it, claim it, expect it, and receive it!

THOUGHT and ACTION EXERCISE #9

Add this affirmation to your list that you made in the previous chapter: I ask for it, visualize it, claim it, expect it, and receive it!

Then, in the space provided, write down three things you want and list some potential ways for how you can get them.

_____
_____
_____
_____
_____
_____

Make a vision board to help you visualize your goals. Tape or glue pictures of the things you want have and that reflect the type of person you want to be on a piece

---

of Bristol board (or on a wall in your bedroom), and look at it each day.

- Use pictures of houses, cars, pools, beaches, etc.
- Arrange them in an aesthetically pleasing way.
- Look at it often!

Then start visualizing yourself getting each thing.

Use meditation to refocus your thoughts and think about what you truly want.

Close your eyes and SEE yourself being successful at getting it. Feel it. Taste it. Touch it.

See yourself achieving each outcome.

Practice this daily.

The more often you practice meditation and visualization, the faster The Law of Attraction will work for you!

Start now, if you can.

- Sit or lie down for 20 minutes.

- Begin with breathing deeply and slowing down your racing thoughts.

- Think of your 3 desires.

- Pick one and focus on it.

-   Use the visualization technique to concentrate on building that scenario in your mind. Add as many details to this mental picture as you can. (If it will help you, you can write out the details in the space below.)

Each time you meditation and practice visualizing your desires, continue to add more and more details until you actually see yourself living as though you have received them!

In time, as you strengthen your new beliefs, they will come true!

_____

_____

_____

_____

_____

_____

_____

_____

_____

_____

_____

_____

_____

_____

_____

_____

_____

Chapter 10: Form Healthy Habits One Step at a Time

When you have suicidal thoughts, you don't have any motivation. You don't want to do much, if anything at all!

Your energy levels are decreased. Just getting through the day is tough.

When you feel this way and are depressed, you might stay in bed all day, you might overeat (or not eat at all), you might fight or have arguments with your friends and/or family members (or those closest to you), and you might not be able to think of anything else other than the thoughts that are consuming you.

When you're feeling like this, you are in a funk, and you can't seem to get out of it.

I know how this feels. I was depressed for years. If I didn't have to do anything, I didn't. Most days, if I didn't have to leave the house, I didn't get dressed. I didn't even shower. I barely moved. I either stayed in bed or on the couch, only getting up to pee, poop, or eat.

I was a wreck, and I knew it.

It wasn't until I was in my forties that I truly learned how to form new habits.

I wish I knew what I know now back then!

However, it's *never* too late to change your bad habits and form new ones. In 2015, when I found out I was diabetic, I knew I had to change my entire lifestyle. I did this one step at a time (and I'm still doing it). I changed my eating habits. I changed my exercising habits. I changed my sleeping habits. I changed my money-saving habits. I also changed my spending habits. As a result, I am happier and healthier!

The key is to identify what needs changing and take one small step at a time to change it. You can't change yourself overnight; growth and self-improvement take time.

> *"The people you surround yourself with influence your behaviors, so choose friends who have healthy habits." ~ Dan Buettner*

I will now share with you some healthy lifestyle habits. Then I will talk about how you can form a new habit.

Habits of a Healthy Lifestyle

1. Eat healthy foods.

2. Eat at regular intervals. This may mean eating 3 bigger meals 4-5 hours apart, or eating 6 smaller meals every 2-3 hours. By eating at regular intervals, you control the amount of sugar and insulin in your blood. You

also control your body's metabolism better if you eat at set times. (Note that it is recommended to eat within the first hour-and-a-half of waking up, to kick-start your metabolism for the day. I learned this when I took a course in 2016 in weight loss and weight management.)

3. Sleep at least 7-8 hours each day.

4. Avoid alcohol consumption that is excessive.

5. Avoid illegal drugs.

6. Exercise. The American Heart Association recommends that you do at least 30 minutes of moderate-intensity aerobic exercises per day, five days a week. You can do this in many ways—by running, dancing, playing a sport, etc. If you choose a fun activity, getting exercise won't feel like a chore!

7. Listen to your body. If you are in pain, treat it. If you are tired, sleep. If you are hungry, eat.

8. Drink a lot of water—8 glasses a day.

9. See a doctor regularly for check-ups. Follow the recommended health checks for all ages and genders that

the CDC (Centers for Disease Control and Prevention) lists on their website.

10. Dress appropriately for the climate you live in. Wear sunscreen when it's sunny, to prevent skin cancer and other diseases. Apply lip balm to your lips to prevent dryness. Wear warm clothing when it is cold out. Dress in layers if you're unsure what to wear!

11. End your unhealthy relationships, if possible. Negative influences and negative people will not help you become a more positive person! If you are in an abusive relationship, there are organizations that will assist you—even going so far as to provide you with food and shelter (for you and your children) and help you start over. Do an Internet search for such organizations in your area.

12. Live within your means and save for your future. Regardless of your earnings, save a small percentage of it each month. Spend wisely. Buy things on sale to help save you money.

13. Limit your use of technology, especially before bedtime. It's been proven that looking at screens prevents you from falling asleep.

14. Incorporate leisure time into each day. You need to have a good work-life balance!

15. Spend time on self-improvement each week.

16. Make goals, and then meet them. (I will help you with this in Chapter 15.)

17. Be social. Spend time with your family and friends whenever possible. If you can't be with them in person, then phone them. If you have Skype or WhatsApp, do a video call with them.

18. Celebrate small wins. When you accomplish something, acknowledge it. Be proud of yourself, and celebrate it!

19. Improve your posture. Stand tall. Sit upright. Don't slouch.

20. Be hygienic. Brush and floss your teeth after eating. Shower or bathe daily. Wash your hands several times a day, especially after you return home from somewhere, after petting a dog or cat, or after doing any activity where you will pick up germs.

21. Set your priorities and execute your tasks in the order of importance and urgency. Make daily To-Do lists and

number your tasks. Then check each task off as you complete it.

22. Practice safe sex or abstinence to avoid STDs (sexually transmitted diseases).

> "We are what we repeatedly do. Excellence, therefore, is not an act but a habit." ~ Aristotle

> "The only proper way to eliminate bad habits is to replace them with good ones." ~ Jerome Hines

How to Change Bad Habits into Good Ones

Studies have shown that it takes 66 days to form a new habit.

It was previously thought to take only 21 days.

"The amount of time it takes for something to become a habit will vary depending on your source of information. Depending on who you ask, you can get answers anywhere from a week to a year. But the most popular answer is 21 days—-postulated in the 1960s

*by Maxwell Maltz, a cosmetic surgeon. But that number was taken as scientific maxim without ever really being tested, until recently. Recent research led by a team at the University College London think they have uncovered just how long (on average) it takes for something to become habitual. They **do not think** it takes 21 days to form a habit. **They believe it takes an average of 66 days to create a habit**." ~ taken from the website called Examined Existence (found at http://examinedexistence.com/how-long-does-it-take-for-something-to-become-a-habit/)*

But… however long it actually takes to form a new habit is irrelevant, because once you have formed a new habit, you will continue to do it!

The key is to start with changing one habit at a time, one small step at a time.

There are several strategies you can use to help you with this:

- ➢ One is by doing a 10-minute daily challenge for 30 days.

- ➢ Another is by creating a reward system for yourself.

- ➢ Another is by simply using a calendar to plan and chart your progress.

However you decide to incorporate changes into your life is up to you, depending on what habits you want to change or start implementing. For example, one of my Facebook friends, who was writing a book, asked me for advice on improving his writing progress.

I said, "Try this technique: write 10 minutes a day as soon as you turn on your computer. It works well."

The following week, he told me he had been using this strategy and that he finished his first chapter!

The reason why it works is because if you tell yourself that you will only do something for 10 minutes, it is a manageable amount of time to commit yourself to, and once you are involved in the activity itself, you don't care how much time has passed. You become more productive as a result!

Creating a reward system worked well for me when I started making changes to my eating and exercise habits. I told myself that if I wanted to eat pizza, I would have to exercise for 30 minutes first. So, I exercised because I love pizza and didn't want to make the sacrifice of not eating it! It was my reward for exercising.

If you decide to use a calendar to help you make changes, you can simply mark the event on the appropriate day(s) and then either use an "X" or a "✓" to denote whether you accomplished it or not.

> *"Achieve success in any area of life by identifying the optimum strategies and repeating them until they become habits."*
> *~ Charles J. Givens*

> *"I never could have done what I have done without the habits of punctuality, order, and diligence, without the determination to concentrate myself on one subject at a time." ~ Charles Dickens*

> *"Successful people are simply those with successful habits." ~ Brian Tracy*

> *"Our character is not so much the product of race and heredity as of those circumstances by which nature forms our habits, by which we are nurtured and live." ~ Marcus Tullius Cicero*

> *"Habits change into character." ~ Ovid*

It is always challenging when you try to make lifestyle changes, or to transform your bad habits into good ones.

You're going to fail a few times before you succeed. This is completely normal, and should be expected. So don't beat yourself up if you "slip up" one day. Forgive yourself.

Let it go.

And move on.

No one is perfect and it is okay to make mistakes!

As long as you put forth a little bit of effort each day, you will see positive results!

THOUGHT and ACTION EXERCISE #10

What are some of your bad habits?

_____

_____

_____

_____

_____

_____

_____

_____

_____

_____

_____

_____

How can you start making changes today to improve them? Fill out the chart provided.

BAD HABIT	ONE THING I CAN DO TO CHANGE IT

Commit to improving yourself by doing one thing *today*.

Write down what you will do. Then do it.

_____

_____

_____

_____

_____

_____

_____

LORRAINE REGULY

Chapter 11: Improve Your Self-Image

When you are suicidal, or have suicidal thoughts, you hate yourself. You hate your life. You might think you are worthless. You might think you are ugly. You might think a dozen other irrational thoughts… that simply are not true.

> *"A strong, positive self-image is the best possible preparation for success." ~ Joyce Brothers*

Most people who are suicidal have a low self-image. I know I did… for years. In fact, some days, I still think I'm not pretty enough or smart enough or helpful enough. These thoughts are irrational. Deep down, I know I am a good person. I know I am intelligent. I know I am helpful to others.

It's normal to have doubts about yourself and your abilities. We just let our insecurities and fears stand in our way. Learning to let go of these things will pave the road to a positive self-image.

How do we change our self-image?

We can do this in various ways! Basically, it boils down to changing your beliefs, which is something I've mentioned several times in this book. By changing your beliefs, you will start seeing yourself in a more positive way!

9 Ways to Change Your Self-Image

1: Observe the way you talk about yourself, and the negative words that you use.

Don't put yourself down. Don't exaggerate. Instead, omit the words with negative connotations from your vocabulary! Change your negative comments into positive ones.

For example, don't tell others "I'm not good at _____" or use the word "never" because these words have a negative effect on your subconscious mind! Instead, put the focus on positive things.

For example, you can say, "I am learning how to improve myself." Do not say, "I will never be smart or rich." You are only sabotaging yourself if you do!

Instead say, "I am going to learn how to increase my income and then apply what I have learned so that I can accomplish my goals."

> *"Our self-image and our habits tend to go together. Change one and you will automatically change the other."*
>
> *~ Napoleon Hill*

2: Replace criticism with encouragement.

Instead of focusing on the negative, replace your self-criticism with encouraging words. Compliment yourself on what you have achieved so far.

For example, instead of saying, "I could have done a better job," say "I did that part well, and I will do a better job next time."

3: Accept your imperfections and don't feel guilty for not being perfect.

No one is perfect. We all have flaws. Instead of trying to be perfect, be realistic, and don't feel bad or guilty!

Think of this: if your car is broken, who would fix it? A chef? No. You would take it to a mechanic!

This is because we each have skill sets that others don't. If you can't do something yourself, get someone to help you. Don't feel bad that you don't know how to fix things yourself. That's why other people exist—to help us!

Focus on what you CAN do instead of what you CAN'T.

4: Be kind to yourself and treat yourself in the same way you would treat others… with respect.

Would you tell your friend she looked "ugly"? Would you tell her that her outfit made her look fat? I doubt it. So why tell yourself these things? Just stop it. Start being a friend to yourself! Respect yourself! You are worthy of it!

5: Don't listen to people who call you names or put you down.

Ignore them. They are only trying to make you feel bad so that they can feel better.

Those types of people have their own issues and limiting beliefs.

You should not care what others think, anyway. What matters is what YOU think.

If you think you are beautiful/handsome, intelligent, and successful, you will feel much better about yourself than if you think you are ugly, stupid, and a failure.

Don't let what others say bother you, if what they are saying is negative.

Instead, eliminate these people from your life. If you can't do that, then each time they try telling you something negative, just cover your ears and say, "I can't hear you!"

Then watch their reaction. They will likely get angry and frustrated… and it serves them right! Laugh at them. Show them that their words are NOT affecting you!

6: Change your environment frequently and help others in the world by doing good deeds.

Don't always stay in one place. Go out. Go for a walk. Go for coffee with a friend.

Look at all the people around you. Watch them and listen to them. Help them if you can.

By changing your environment, you will see that you are not really that bad off... there are many other people in this world who have it worse than you do.

This is one strategy that always makes me feel better about myself.

I live in a city that gets very cold in the winter, and I sometimes don't like going out because of the weather. (The temperature gets as low as minus 35 degrees Celsius!) But when I *do* go out, I encounter people and situations that make me realize how lucky I am.

I don't have a car, so I either rely on others for rides, take the city bus, hire a taxi, or walk.

If I take a bus, I'm often approached at the bus terminal while switching buses. Some people have asked me for bus fare or cigarettes. If I have change (money) on me, I will give them bus fare. If I only have a bus-punch pass with me, I will let the bus driver punch my pass, thereby paying their bus fare.

Some people sit outside with signs that say "Need food" or "Help me." I have seen such people outside drugstores, banks, and our local casino. I have given these people money and/or food. I have also seen a busker—a guy who sings and plays a guitar for money—and I have donated to him, too. In fact, I got to know him. He is now my friend, and we have hung out together!

It's sad to see people less fortunate than I am, and I help them whenever I can. Even though I have credit card debt, and technically cannot really afford to help others financially, I help them anyway! I am the type of person who does not like to see others starve.

It also makes me appreciate what I have.

In addition, by helping others, or doing good deeds, you will feel better about yourself. You will feel happy and proud. You are also sending out good karma into the Universe when you do such acts! Good things will happen to you as a result!

7: Improve or enhance your home environment.

If you have a nice visual display of yourself and your home, you will feel more positive.

Clean your house often. Tidy things up and get rid of the clutter. Wash your own clothes. Straighten your desk. Organize your drawers, cupboards, and closets.

You will feel a sense of satisfaction and pride if you do these things yourself.

Your mood will be improved and you will feel better.

8: Invest in yourself.

Read self-improvement books, listen to motivational podcasts and audiobooks, and watch inspirational videos. Take a class to learn a new skill. Attend a seminar.

By improving your skills and expanding your knowledge, you will become a better person. Ultimately, your self-image will improve!

9: Smile and laugh a lot.

I am a very serious person. As a result, I don't laugh or smile enough!

I know this is one of my flaws or imperfections, and so I have learned to talk to friends who always make me laugh. I also watch funny sitcoms and stand-up comedy routines to add laughter to my life.

Sometimes I even play with children (such as my niece and nephew). Kids can be hilarious with the things they say and do!

I'm sure you've heard the saying that "laughter is the best medicine," right? It's true!

You can't be sad if you are laughing!

The same principle applies to smiling. When you smile, you feel good. You feel happy. You feel positive.

Smile right now. Please. Just do it! You'll see what I mean! (Come on, do it... no one is watching!)

I used to be very self-conscious about smiling because I had bad teeth. I had an overbite, too. Other people said they liked my smile, but I didn't like it at all.

Over the years, my teeth worsened and I started experiencing pain in my jaw. I went to the dentist and he examined me. He told me that I had two options: I could have some root canal done to fix my teeth or I could have them all removed and get false teeth. He told me that I would need dentures one day anyway, so I decided to have my teeth removed. I was only 22 at the time.

When they made my dentures, they fixed my overbite issues. Now that my teeth are fixed, I am not afraid to smile anymore. I know my smile is nice!

More importantly, I feel good when I smile.

Smile again now! (This time, I'm watching you!)

See the effect? I know you feel just a bit better now!

Now that you are smiling, I want you to take some time to do the Thought and Action Exercise for this chapter. As you complete it, remember to smile. It will help you shift your thoughts to positive ones!

THOUGHT and ACTION EXERCISE #11

What are some of your good qualities?

List them.

_____

_____

_____

_____

_____

_____

_____

_____

_____

_____

_____

_____

_____

_____

Now try to re-define yourself. Write down the type of person you want to be. List as many qualities as you can.

_____

_____

_____

_____

_____

_____
_____
_____
_____
_____
_____
_____
_____
_____
_____
_____
_____
_____
_____
_____

Then review the 9 ways to change your self-image and list the ways you know will help you. By writing them down, it will help you to solidify them in your brain!

_____
_____
_____
_____
_____
_____
_____
_____
_____
_____
_____
_____
_____

_____
_____
_____
_____
_____

Do one thing today from that list.

Do another tomorrow.

Do something from this list each day this week! (You can print this out and keep it handy to remind yourself of what to do, too.)

Write down your plan for this week.

_____
_____
_____
_____
_____
_____
_____
_____
_____
_____
_____
_____
_____
_____
_____
_____

LORRAINE REGULY

Chapter 12: Alternative Treatments and Counselling

Up to this point, I have taught you:

> ➢ temporary and long-term coping strategies you can use (in Chapter 6)

> ➢ how to identify your emotions and release negativity from your life (in Chapter 7)

> ➢ how to change your mindset by using positive affirmations (in Chapter 8)

> ➢ how to use meditation, the Law of Attraction, and visualization (in Chapter 9)

> ➢ how to form healthy habits one step at a time (in Chapter 10)

> ➢ how to improve your self-image (in Chapter 11)

There are more things I am going to teach you, too, in this as well as later chapters. However, regardless of how many different techniques and coping strategies you use, there is a big probability that you will not address the root cause of your problems.

There is a high chance that you have deep-rooted issues that I simply cannot help you with. For this reason, I highly recommend that you seek professional counselling.

During my lifetime, I have spoken with several medical professionals.

I have seen psychologists, a psychometrist, a psychiatrist, and other professional counsellors.

Each has helped me in his or her own way. I underwent various assessments and was also prescribed a variety medications.

Medical professionals have access to resources that I do not. They possess specific knowledge that I do not. Some of them can also advise you to take—and prescribe to you—medications, which I cannot.

Therefore, it is imperative that you seek some type of help from such people.

There could be costs involved in seeking such help. I was fortunate in that my government funded many of the programs in which I participated. You might not be as lucky. So what are you to do?

What are the alternatives?

First of all, you can buy, read, and use some self-help books.

The Courage to Heal Textbook and The Courage to Heal Workbook helped me a lot in overcoming the sexual abuse I endured. My ex-boyfriend used it to help him deal with the abuse his adoptive parents inflicted upon him. The exercises in it are multi-purposeful.

If you need to deal with specific traumas you have endured, you can search for books on "how to overcome grief," "how to overcome addiction," "how to deal with tragedy," or whatever topic it is that you need help with. Check Chapter 21 for additional resources and books I recommend.

Secondly, you can also access free resources from different websites that might help you deal with some of your issues.

There is one particular website, created by a woman who suffered from both depression and suicidal thoughts, that provides free access to a ton of resources she developed herself.

This woman is Byron Katie. Her website is called The Work. She gives you all the tools you need to do The Work (for free). She guides you through different exercises you can do and provides step-by-step assistance for you to identify and work through your problems. She also provides various videos for you to watch and learn from, and answers a lot of FAQs (frequently asked questions).

She really is quite amazing! She is an acclaimed author, too, and her books are available through her website as well as from Amazon.

Here is a bit of information for you, taken directly from her website page about her:

"Byron Katie, founder of The Work, has one job: to teach people how to end their own suffering. As she guides people through the powerful process of inquiry she calls The Work, they find that their stressful beliefs— about life, other people, or themselves— radically shift and their lives are changed forever. Based on Byron Katie's direct experience of how suffering is created and ended, The Work is an astonishingly simple process, accessible to people of all ages and backgrounds, and requires nothing more than a pen, paper, and an open mind.

Through this process, anyone can learn to trace unhappiness to its source and deal with it there. Katie (as everyone calls her) not only shows us that all the problems in the world originate in our thinking: she gives us the tool to open our minds and set ourselves free."

(http://thework.com/en/about-byron-katie)

Some of the books she has written include:

- *Peace in the Present Moment*

- *Who Would You Be Without Your Story?*

- *Question Your Thinking, Change the World*

- *I Need Your Love—Is That True?*

- *Loving What Is: Four Questions That Can Change Your Life*

- *A Friendly Universe*

Thirdly, you can use some of the other methods and techniques taught online to ease your pain. They won't delve deep into your psyche like a counsellor would, but they are available as alternative treatments.

> *"Courage doesn't happen when you have all the answers. It happens when you are ready to face the questions you have been avoiding your whole life."* ~ *Shannon L. Alder*

> *"Let your past be your spring-board, not your quicksand."* ~ *Dr. Steve Maraboli*

Two Other Methods and Techniques You Can Use to Ease Your Pain:

There are two techniques you can use at home that involves touching various pressure points on your body that releases any negativity you may be feeling.

These two methods are The Sedona Method and EFT Tapping.

The Sedona Method is, according to their website, *"a unique, simple, powerful, easy-*

to-learn and duplicate technique that shows you how to uncover your natural ability to let go of any painful or unwanted feeling in the moment. The Sedona Method consists of a series of questions you ask yourself that lead your awareness to what you are feeling in the moment and gently guide you into the experience of letting go."

(http://www.sedona.com/What-Is-The-Sedona-Method.asp)

While this method is simply demonstrated through a video found on that page, there is also a course you can take to learn more about it.

However, some free information about this method is provided on their website. It's up to you to decide if this method is right for you.

The second alternative treatment you can use to improve your well-being is the EFT tapping technique.

According to the EmoFree website: *"Emotional Freedom Techniques, or EFT (often known as Tapping or EFT Tapping), is a universal healing tool that can provide impressive results for physical, emotional, and performance issues. EFT operates on the premise that no matter what part of your life needs improvement, there are unresolved emotional issues in the way. Even for physical issues, chronic pain, or diagnosed conditions, it is common knowledge that any kind of emotional stress can impede the natural healing potential of the human body."*

(https://www.emofree.com/eft-tutorial/tapping-basics/what-is-eft.html)

Their article titled "How to do EFT Tapping—The Basic Tapping Procedure" explains the steps in-depth.

They also provide a video for you to watch.

In fact, there are many websites dedicated to teaching this technique.

The EFT Mercola site provides a tutorial too, and states:

"EFT is easy to learn and will help you:

- remove negative emotions

- reduce food cravings

- reduce or eliminate pain

- implement positive goals"

(http://eft.mercola.com/)

This particular website outlines the tapping locations on your body, the EFT technique, how to find the right tapping points, how to use affirmation statements, tips and tricks for using advanced affirmation statements, how to practice your affirmation statements with timing and mirror work, and alternative approaches and final recommendations.

You can easily read about these things online and learn them for free.

Summary

Seeking counselling is a personal choice. Exploring different treatment options is too.

I can say with certainty that counselling helped me.

I have also tried alternative treatments to assist me in alleviating my pain.

It is up to you to try various methods until you find one that works for you.

I have provided you with many options in this chapters. I sincerely hope you explore them!

THOUGHT and ACTION EXERCISE #12

In the spaces provided, answer the following questions:

While you were reading about the alternative treatments and counselling suggestions, which ones did you find most appealing?

_____

_____

_____
_____
_____
_____
_____

Which method do you want to try?

_____
_____
_____
_____

Make it a point of trying the EFT Tapping technique.

Once you have tried it, record how you felt afterward.

_____
_____
_____
_____
_____
_____
_____
_____

Do some research in your city or town and find out how to get a counsellor.

Make an appointment with one, then go. Do not cancel the appointment.

Get an assessment done by a professional. Perhaps medication is something you need. Be open to such solutions.

Record your thoughts on this topic. Are you afraid of seeking counselling? Are you worried you might need medication? By analyzing your thoughts, you might gain some insight about yourself.

Record your insights, too.

_____

_____

_____

_____

_____

_____

_____

_____

_____

_____

_____

_____

_____

_____

Chapter 13: Acceptance, Spirituality, and Your Will to Change

Because you are reading this book, it is clear that you have a will (a desire) to change.

Congratulations on making it this far! You're doing great!

I am proud of you for taking these important steps to change your life, and I sincerely hope you are learning a lot and becoming a more positive, hope-filled person.

I also hope you are completing the exercises that accompany each chapter, because that is where the true value of this book lies: in thinking and taking action!

Your suicidal thoughts are simply not going to disappear by themselves. You need to take certain actions and make changes in your life to rid yourself of them.

The many strategies and techniques mentioned in this book are designed to help you do just that. If you understand the way your brain works, you are more likely to re-train it in a positive way. You learned how to do this in Chapters 8 and 9.

If you understand that there is a connection between how you think and what you believe, you are more likely to act with purpose, in a more positive manner.

Once you have a deeper understanding of these things, your wisdom and acceptance will increase. You will realize that there are things you simply cannot change, and you will have more knowledge regarding changing the things you *can*.

Connected within all of this is the concept of spirituality and peace. After all, ridding yourself of your pain and your negative thoughts and finding peace within yourself is what you are ultimately striving toward!

But I do not simply want you to eliminate your suicidal thoughts from your life. I want you to become a better, happier, more successful person. In fact, I want you to become the best version of yourself that you can be!

Living our lives to the fullest is something most people do not do! Therefore, it is vital for us to understand why we behave the way we do, and what motivates us to do so.

The most famous theory regarding this topic was invented by Abraham Maslow (1908-1970), an American psychologist and psychology professor, who stressed the importance of focusing on the positive qualities of people. Maslow also created the famed Hierarchy of Needs, most often used and remembered for its visual representation of a pyramid.

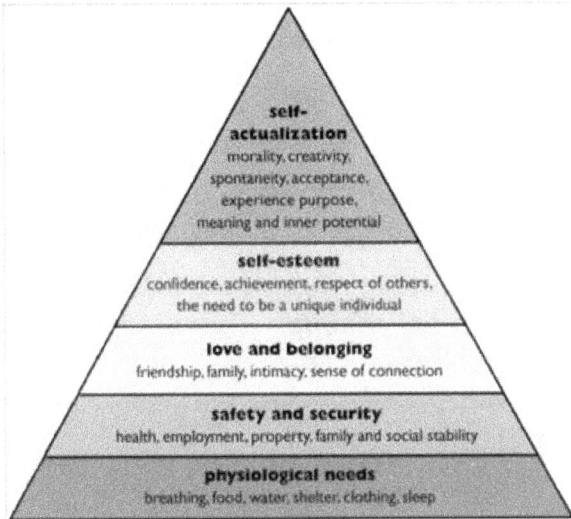

self-
actualization
morality, creativity,
spontaneity, acceptance,
experience purpose,
meaning and inner potential

self-esteem
confidence, achievement, respect of others,
the need to be a unique individual

love and belonging
friendship, family, intimacy, sense of connection

safety and security
health, employment, property, family and social stability

physiological needs
breathing, food, water, shelter, clothing, sleep

We should all strive to move up the pyramid to reach self-actualization!

From reading this book and learning the different things you have learned, you are one step closer.

You've learned how to improve your confidence and self-esteem from reading Chapter 11: Improve Your Self-Image. In Chapters 14 and 15, you will learn more strategies that will help you climb to the top.

Each positive action you take in your life will move you one step closer to experiencing feelings of purpose and meaning!

In the last 50 years, there have been some changes to Maslow's five-stage hierarchy. Both a seven-stage and an eight-stage model have been developed.

According to the website Simply Psychology, the eight-stage hierarchy is as follows:

1. **Biological and Physiological needs** *(air, food, drink, shelter, warmth, sex, sleep, etc.)*

2. **Safety needs** *(protection from elements, security, order, law, stability, etc.)*

3. **Love and belongingness needs** *(friendship, intimacy, trust and acceptance, receiving and giving affection and love, affiliating, being part of a group [family, friends, work], etc.)*

4. **Esteem needs** *(self-esteem, achievement, independence, status, dominance, prestige, managerial responsibility, mastery, etc.)*

5. **Cognitive needs** *(knowledge and understanding, curiosity, exploration, need for meaning and predictability, etc.)*

6. **Aesthetic needs** *(appreciation and search for beauty, balance, form, etc.)*

7. ***Self-Actualization needs*** *(realizing personal potential, self-fulfillment, seeking personal growth and peak experiences, etc.)*

8. ***Transcendence needs*** *(helping others to achieve self-actualization.*

This summary was taken from the article titled "Maslow's Hierarchy of Needs, found at https://www.simplypsychology.org/maslow.html.

That article also states that *"Every person is capable and has the desire to move up the hierarchy toward a level of self-actualization. Unfortunately, progress is often disrupted by a failure to meet lower level needs. Life experiences, including divorce and loss of a job may cause an individual to fluctuate between levels of the hierarchy. Therefore, not everyone will move through the hierarchy in a uni-directional manner but may move back and forth between the different types of needs."*

I am sure that as you looked through each of the tiers of the hierarchy, you saw yourself fitting into several of the levels, to some extent.

I know I did!

I believe I am on a path to self-actualization, even though it is estimated that less than 2%

of the world's population actually reach this level!

Some days, given the depression I suffer from, it's simply enough for me for make it through the day!

But it is good to have goals and a desire to be a better person. I have these. I am also sure you do, too. (If you are interested in learning more about self-actualization or the qualities of self-actualized people, there is a ton of free information available on the Internet. You can do this extra research and learn on your own, as there is only so much I can teach you here!)

Because Maslow's original hierarchy has been altered to include transcendence, it is important to note its definition, because *transcendence* is different from *self-transcendence.*

Transcendence is defined as the state of excelling or surpassing or going beyond usual limits.

Self-transcendence is defined as the overcoming of the limits of the individual self and its desires in spiritual contemplation and realization.

More simply put, it is the ability to focus your attention on doing something for the sake of others, as opposed to self-actualization, in which doing something for yourself is an end goal.

These two pertain to your acceptance and your will to change because of the potential you have within yourself, not only to be the best you can be, but also to help others in the process.

You are capable of doing more than you know or can imagine!

You are also capable of overcoming any hardships you might face. All you need is the desire to do so!

If you possess this desire, then nothing will stop you from learning and improving yourself.

I know, because I am at this point in my life right now. I have been improving myself and helping others to do the same.

It's also never too late to start making changes in your life, nor is it ever too late to learn something new.

Learning is lifelong. That is one of the awesome things about our lives! However, you need to understand that there are certain things you simply cannot change in this world.

This point reminds me of **The Serenity Prayer**, which says:

"Grant me the serenity to accept the things I cannot change; courage to change the things I can; and wisdom to know the difference."

Stop for a moment and read that again.

Let it sink in.

Perhaps you have heard of this verse before. The Serenity Prayer was originally written by the American theologian Reinhold Niebuhr (1892–1971). It was popularized by Alcoholics Anonymous and other 12-step programs, and is used worldwide.

While I am not about to preach religion to you, I wanted to share this with you because it is so profound.

There are many things in our lives that are simply out of our control, things we cannot change. And there are certain things we actually *do* have the power to change.

Distinguishing between these two is what ultimately helps us to make positive changes in our lives. Once we realize what we can and cannot change, life becomes easier to handle and our problems become easier to deal with. As a result, we end up acquiring a peacefulness and an acceptance in our lives which we never had before.

That is part of what spirituality does for us: it gives us peace.

Again, I'm not going to preach religion to you. There are many religions in this world. Each has their own merit, and I don't want to say that one is better than the other.

I respect each person for having his or her own religious or spiritual beliefs. However, because the main focus of this book involves changing your belief systems to become a more positive and productive person, it is important to mention spirituality here.

> *"There is only one dream that will always be perfect in your lifetime, and that is the dream of self-transcendence." ~ Sri Chinmoy*

Spirituality has different meanings to everyone, and there is no single, widely agreed upon definition of this term, but it basically involves the following components:

- the values and meanings by which we live

- a personal relationship with your "Higher Power" (God, Allah, the Universe, or whichever name you use for your Higher Power)

- a belief that there is something greater than you out there, whether it's the supernatural, or something else beyond what is known and observable

- a quest for the meaning of life

- growth and transformation or re-formation

- self-transcendence

Being spiritual is different from being religious. For example, I was raised in the Roman Catholic religion, but I do not believe everything that is taught in that religion. As a result, I do not go to church, and I have formed my own personal set of beliefs.

I don't consider myself to be religious, but I do consider myself to be somewhat spiritual.

There is an acronym for people such as myself, who don't attend church but consider themselves spiritual beings: SBNR.

SBNR stands for *spiritual but not religious*.

I believe there is a higher power who is all-knowing and all-seeing, and I believe in treating others the way I want to be treated.

I have private conversations with my higher power sometimes. Sometimes I pray too. I have even spoken to people who have died, such as some of my family members. Of course, they don't talk back to me, but I like to think they can hear me. Plus, during the writing of this book, I spoke to the sister of the guy who wrote Chapter 20: The After-

Effects of Suicide: DK's Story of His Sister. I asked her to give him the strength to write.

DK and I were communicating via Facebook Messenger private messages. He told me of his sister's death shortly after she died. As I neared the completion of this book, I thought it would be a good idea to have him share his story. He agreed, but writing it all down was very difficult for him (understandably!).

So, what we did was this: we texted each other via messages, with me asking him personal questions and him writing replies. I took all of his messages and combined them to create the final chapter for this book. Of course, I sent it to him first, to show him the order and make sure it was the way he wanted it presented.

We did this over a series of days. It was not easy, for either one of us. I cried a lot during this process. He did, too.

I felt his pain, and I urged him to continue despite how difficult it was. I remember sending him one message, telling him to simply *breathe*. This is good advice for all of us!

I still cry when I read DK's story. In fact, I am starting to tear up now, just thinking about it.

Why did DK and I put ourselves through this? Because I believe it is important for you to know and hear about how someone's suicide affects others!

That is why I helped DK tell his story.

How can you strengthen your spirituality?

There are several ways you can do this:

- meditate

- pray

- practice mindfulness (according to Wikipedia, mindfulness is defined as "the psychological process of bringing one's attention to the internal and external experiences occurring in the present moment")

- read sacred texts (such as the Bible, the Koran, the Bhagavad Gita, etc.)

- have conversations with your higher power

- have conversations with people who have died

- do Yoga, which is a Hindu spiritual and ascetic discipline involving a set of mental and physical exercises aimed at producing spiritual enlightenment as well as improved health and relaxation. There are many videos on YouTube that will show you what to do.

- you can also attend religious services at churches, Temples, Mosques, or whichever place of worship you desire to attend.

- listen to music

"We can no more do without spirituality than we can do without food, shelter, or clothing." ~ Ernest Holmes

By strengthening your spirituality, you will gain feelings of peacefulness in your life.

This will cause you to be a more accepting, understanding person, and will help lead you toward a path of happiness.

This is only one step you can take to creating a path to a happier life. In the next few chapters, you will learn other things you can do to make this happen.

THOUGHT and ACTION EXERCISE #13

Answer the following questions in the space provided.

Which tiers do you fall into in the hierarchy of needs?

At which level do you think you will be happy?

Are you a spiritual person?

How can you strengthen your spirituality?

_____

_____

_____

_____

_____

_____

_____

_____

_____

_____

_____

_____

_____

_____

_____

_____

_____

_____

_____

_____

_____

_____

_____

_____

FROM NOPE TO HOPE

Chapter 14: Create Your Path to a Happier Life

> *"Happiness is not something ready-made. It comes from your own actions." ~ Dalai Lama*

As I mentioned in Chapter 13, strengthening your spirituality is only one step you can take to create a more peaceful, happier life for yourself.

Although the majority of this book has mentioned different techniques you can use to improve your mood, there are a few more things you can do to create a happier life for yourself. Most require very little effort, too!

Here is a list of 17 things you can easily do:

1: Make doing your chores fun and/or educational. You can do this by listening to music or a podcast. Most people view chores as "work" (which is not usually fun to do), but if you listen to music as you do these tasks, you will be happier while you do them.

2: You can get dressed up, even if you have nowhere to go. When you look good, you feel good. Most people know that! (If you're female, put on some make-up. Do your hair. Shave your legs. Put on a dress. Make yourself look and feel pretty.

If you're male, have a shower, wash your hair, and put on some cologne. Shave too, unless you have a beard. Put on a suit. Make yourself smell and feel good!)

By donning some of your nicer clothing, your mood will improve. Consequently, you will feel like finding somewhere to go or doing something productive. Either way, you'll be happier than if you didn't do these things!

I know I feel better when I "dress for the office" even though I work from home. It's true that there have been days when I have stayed in my pajamas all day, but I have found that I am more productive when I am fully dressed. I also like dressing up. It makes me feel like I am important. (I know I'm important, but I don't always FEEL important. There's a difference!)

3: Pamper yourself. You can do this in many different ways. For example, you can get a massage, take a candlelit bubble bath (perhaps while drinking a glass of wine or reading a novel), or you can make your favorite meal and enjoy it in the company of a family member or close friend. You can also go out for dinner to your favorite restaurant, spend time on one of your hobbies, or do any other activity that you don't normally do every day.

The key is to treat yourself like a king or queen.

4: Play a game. You can do this in several ways, either alone or with family members or friends.

With others, you can play some type of a board game such as Checkers, Chess, Monopoly or Clue, or you can play card games. You can create a game of your own, too!

Alone, you can play video games online, or you can download some games to your smartphone. There are many games on Facebook, and even more on Google Play. These games include different types of puzzles, too.

Experiment with different ones until you find something you enjoy playing!

In my life, I play cards with my mom and dad. We make things more interesting because we play for money. Even though this is technically gambling, the money stays within our family. I like playing cards with my parents not only because I enjoy the game, but also because it allows us to spend time together. They are not going to be alive forever, and so I cherish the fun moments we have.

When I am alone, I sometimes play games on my phone. I actually like doing this as a way to relax. I find that the constant repetition of slot/casino-type games allows me to shift my thoughts from work to other things.

Sometimes I like simply not thinking at all! I also like playing the "bonus" games on some of the game applications installed on my phone. It's fun trying to beat your high score or making it to the top prize!

5: Chat with your friends. You can do this in several ways. Phone someone. Text someone. Go out for coffee. Visit someone, or invite them to your house. Talking to someone always helps!

6. Masturbate or have sex. Seriously, I'm not kidding! Allow yourself to enjoy the moment, and release some of your tension. It works!

7: Be unique; don't compare yourself to others. Focus on your own journey.

> *"Don't let anyone tell you that you have to be a certain way. Be unique." ~ Melissa Etheridge*

8: Don't take anything for granted. Be grateful for what you have. Many others have much less than you.

> *"Gratitude helps you to grow and expand; gratitude brings joy and laughter into your life and into the lives of all those around you." ~ Eileen Caddy*

> *"It isn't what you have, or who you are, or where you are, or what you are doing that makes you happy or unhappy. It is what you think about."* ~ Dale Carnegie

9: Think positive thoughts.

> *"Very little is needed to make a happy life; it is all within yourself, in your way of thinking."* ~ Marcus Aurelius

> *"A happy person is not a person in a certain set of circumstances, but rather a person with a certain set of attitudes."* ~ Hugh Downs

10: Stay positive and keep going. Never give up. Remember, things could be much worse than they are!

> *"Stay positive and happy. Work hard and don't give up hope. Be open to criticism and keep learning. Surround yourself with happy, warm and genuine people."* ~ Tena Desae

11: Make the most of each moment!

> *"Learn to enjoy every minute of your life. Be happy now. Don't wait for something outside of yourself to make you happy in*

> *the future. Think how really precious is the time you have to spend, whether it's at work or with your family. Every minute should be enjoyed and savored." ~ Earl Nightingale*

> *"Be happy for this moment. This moment is your life." ~ Omar Khayyam*

12: Listen to music. Music has the ability to heal you and to make you feel happy.

> *"Music is a moral law. It gives soul to the universe, wings to the mind, flight to the imagination, and charm and gaiety to life and to everything." ~ Plato*

> *"Music is the universal language of mankind." ~ Henry Wadsworth Longfellow*

> *"Without music, life would be a mistake." ~ Friedrich Nietzche*

> *"Music is therapy. Music moves people. It connects people in ways that no other medium can. It pulls heart strings. It acts as medicine." ~ Macklemore*

13: Dance! Dance while cooking and cleaning, either alone or with others! It's fun!

14: Believe in yourself.

> *"Believe in yourself! Have faith in your abilities! Without a humble but reasonable confidence in your own powers you cannot be successful or happy." ~ Norman Vincent Peale*

15: Smile. Do this often. The effects of a single smile are tremendous!

> *"Whoever is happy will make others happy too." ~ Anne Frank*

16: Read motivational quotes. They help improve your mood. They also get you thinking in the right direction.

> *"Happiness is a choice. You can choose to be happy. There's going to be stress in life, but it's your choice whether you let it affect you or not." ~ Valerie Bertinelli*

17: Laugh. Laugh each day.

This last piece of advice is particularly difficult for me. Because I am such a serious person all of the time, it takes a lot of effort for me to find things to laugh at. I tend to watch sitcoms and so I usually laugh at the really funny ones, but I've found that this is not enough.

To add more laughter to my life, I talk to certain people who have the ability to make me laugh. I also sometimes read jokes. Whenever I talk to or see my sister's small children, I laugh at them. Kids can be hilarious in what they say and do! Their laughs are also infectious, and so playing games or tickling them immediately improves my serious mood!

> *"Laughter is an instant vacation." ~ Milton Berle*

> *"Let us be grateful to people who make us happy, they are the charming gardeners who make our souls blossom." ~ Marcel Proust*

> *"A day without laughter is a day wasted." ~ Charlie Chaplin*

Understand What Happiness Really Is

Being happy is different from deriving pleasure from something. Although it's a good idea to find activities that you enjoy doing, and do at least one every day, it's important to understand that "pleasure is momentary and is dependent on circumstance. Happiness is something more constant and internal. You do not feel it because a certain condition was satisfied but rather because you are satisfied with your current state." This was taken from an article written by Noel Ross, on the website Life's How You Live It, titled "4 Things You Should Know About Happiness."

(http://lifeshowyouliveit.com/happiness/)

It's also important to know that happiness is not an outcome.

In the same Internet article I just mentioned, Noel Ross also states, "Happiness isn't conditional. You can be happy no matter what kind of circumstances you're going through."

Another Internet article, "10 Things You Should Know About Creating Your Happiness" agrees, as it asserts that you don't need to have an easy life to be happy. This article also states that happiness comes from within.

The best article on happiness that I found is "10 Important Things You Should Know About Happiness." It is found on the Truth Theory website. I highly suggest reading it. It offers excellent insights into what happiness really is.

Happiness is not a myth; it is a state of mind. It involves your thoughts, your beliefs, and your actions. It's up to you to create happiness for yourself! It might take you some time to do this, and you might never feel happy 100% of the time, but is simply how life goes. Life gives you challenges, and you have to overcome them. However, it is important to realize that we need to know sadness so we can appreciate our happiness that much more!

> *"Life is so ironic. It takes sadness to know happiness, noise to appreciate silence, and absence to value presence." ~ Author Unknown*

Each of us experiences moments of happiness, but the key is to look at your life as a big picture. If you can say that you are happy with the different areas of your life, then you are doing great! At the time of this writing, I can honestly say I am about 85-90% happy with my current life, with the relationships I have with others, with my spirituality, with how I fill my days, with what my habits are, and with all of the successes I have and the progress I have made during my life's journey.

I've learned to create a good work-life balance for myself, and have developed routines that help me stay on track.

> *"The happiness of your life depends upon the quality of your thoughts..." ~ Marcus Aurelius*

I wrote a blog post about this topic, too, and created a free planner you can use to help you too. You can get access to it for free from the link in the article on Wording Well titled "How to Find a Good Work-Life Balance (+ a FREE Workbook/Planner)."

Creating a happy life for yourself not only involves finding balance within it, but also creating a plan for yourself in which you set goals and work towards achieving them.

Goal-setting will be discussed in the next chapter!

For now, remember that happiness is personal and it is up to you create your path to a happier life, using the techniques and ideas which I have given you!

THOUGHT and ACTION EXERCISE #14

How are you going to create your path to happiness?

Which of the 17 things listed in this chapter are you going to do?

Write them in the space provided.

_____
_____
_____
_____
_____

Chapter 15: Put Your Plan into Action by Setting and Attaining Goals

The problem most people have is that they don't know how to move forward or make positive changes to their lives. You are lucky. You have this book to help you!

You know how to change your mindset and become a more positive person (because of the positive affirmations discussed in Chapter 8). You know how to use visualization to get what you want (because of the meditation and visualization techniques discussed in Chapter 9).

You have started forming healthy habits (because you read Chapter 10). You've improved your self-image (because you read Chapter 11).

You've explored alternative treatments and counselling (because you read Chapter 12).

You've increased your acceptance, spirituality, and inner peacefulness (because you read Chapter 13).

You've learned how to create your path to a happier life (because you read Chapter 14). And now you are going to learn how to take the steps necessary to create and achieve your goals!

The Types of Goals

There are two types of goals: short-term goals and long-term goals.

Short-term goals are those that can be attained in a short amount of time. They are small things that are usually fairly easy to accomplish.

Some examples of short-term goals are:

> ➢ having a shower
> ➢ cleaning the house
> ➢ saving $100
> ➢ losing 5 pounds

Long-term goals are bigger and take careful planning.

Some examples of long-term goals are:

> ➢ Starting a business
> ➢ Buying a house
> ➢ Saving $1000
> ➢ Losing 50 pounds

For people who suffer from suicidal thoughts or depression, the process of creating and reaching even *just one goal* can be a daunting task. I know, because when I was suffering from depression and spent days on end in bed, the task of taking a shower and getting dressed seemed like an impossible feat.

I would sometimes go days without showering because it would take all of my energy to drag myself out of bed and bathe myself. However, each time I managed to do it, I felt better! Being clean and refreshed elevated my mood, each and every time! I knew this would be the result, too, yet I still had problems taking that first step…

Taking that first step is one of the reasons more people are not as successful or as happy as they want to be.

It's tough to take that first step, regardless of what you are taking it toward.

And if you don't have any set goals to work toward, you are merely existing and not living life to its fullest! The solution, therefore, is to set some goals and work toward them.

> *"There are different paths to your destination. Choose your own path." ~ Lailah Gifty Akita*

How to Set Goals:

1. Think of something you want to accomplish.

   Think of many different things!

2. Write them down.

3. List the action steps you need to take in order to reach each goal. (For bigger goals, there will be more steps involved. Focus on one step at a time!)

Revise wherever necessary, whenever necessary, and seek help when you need it.

> *"When it is obvious that the goals cannot be reached, don't adjust the goals, adjust the action steps." ~ Confucius*

> *"People with goals succeed because they know where they're going." ~ Earl Nightingale*

When you are listing the steps involved to reach your goals, remember these 3 simple rules of life:

1. If you do NOT go after what you want you will NEVER have it.

2. If you do NOT ask, the answer will always be NO.

3. If you do NOT step forward, you will ALWAYS be in the same place making the same mistakes (or amount of money), with the same problems weighing you down.

> *"Crystallize your goals. Make a plan for achieving them and set yourself a*

> *deadline. Then, with supreme confidence, determination, and disregard for obstacles and other people's criticisms, carry out your plan." ~ Paul J. Meyer*

In the book, *You Can Win*, written by Shiv Khera (which you will remember helped Farhan tremendously!), there is a section that explains why more people don't set goals.

Here is the excerpt:

"Why don't more people set goals?

1. *A pessimistic attitude*
2. *Fear of failure*
3. *A lack of ambition*
4. *A fear of rejection*
5. *Procrastination*
6. *Low self-esteem*
7. *Ignorance of the importance of goal setting*
8. *A lack of knowledge about goal-setting"*

Fortunately for you, you are learning how to combat these many obstacles by reading the different chapters of this book!

> *"Try not to become a man of success, but rather try to become a man of value." ~ Albert Einstein*

To increase your knowledge about goal-setting, I want to tell you about SMART goals.

SMART goals are:

S—Specific, significant

M—Measurable, meaningful, motivational

A—Achievable, attainable, action-oriented

R—Realistic, reasonable, relevant, and

rewarding

T—Timely, tangible, trackable

Most goals you set will be considered SMART goals. For more information on SMART goals and how to create them, you can read the Internet article titled "Creating S.M.A.R.T. Goals" and its companion article "Goal Setting—Powerful Written Goals in 7 Easy Steps!"

There are different ways you can track your goals, too. You can use a simple checklist. You can use a computer or phone app. You can any of the tools listed in the Internet articles titled "9 Great Tools for Achieving Your Goals" or "Tools to Help You Set, Track and Achieve Your Goals."

One phone app that you can use for setting and tracking your goals is **Way of Life 3** and is available for both iPhone and Android phones. This app has many useful features. It includes a walk-through tutorial, a passcode lock, and the ability to connect with Dropbox.

You can also create a spreadsheet for your goals. If you don't have Microsoft Excel (spreadsheet software), you can sign up for a Google/Gmail account and get free access to Google Sheets.

Depending on what your goals are, you might face some obstacles. However, you can find ways to overcome these obstacles.

For example, when I decided to lose weight, I knew I'd have an issue with eating while I watched TV, because I like "munching" while engaging in such an activity. To overcome this obstacle, I did a few things. I recognized that I had a problem. I switched the food I ate from unhealthy (potato chips) to healthy (carrot sticks and nuts). Instead of sitting on the couch, I sat on the floor and did exercises (stretches, leg lifts, etc.).

Obstacles are not hard things to change. They are simply minor problems that have solutions. It's up to you to find the solutions that will work for you.

One thing to remember is to keep your goals in mind at all times. Keep your list of goals handy and review them each day and each week. Track your progress, and with each action you take and each decision you make, ask yourself if you are moving in the right direction.

Rachit Singh (AKA Writard on YouTube), talks about the importance of setting goals in his one of his YouTube videos, titled "Importance of Goal Setting—SL EP03."

He says, "A goal is like travelling with a map. If you don't have a map, you will either get lost or wander all your life entertaining others."

This quote speaks volumes to me because it's so true. Anytime I have travelled, I have always used a map. I like knowing where I am going, and I like knowing how I will get there.

I like this "map" analogy with respect to goal-setting because your list of action steps serves as the "map" you need to reach your goals. That is why it is so important to not just create a goal, but to list the steps necessary in order to attain that goal. Once you have set some goals for yourself and started the process of achieving them, you will feel better about yourself, and take pride in yourself for moving forward.

By having something positive to focus on, your suicidal thoughts will dissipate, and you will start enjoying your journey to self-fulfillment.

The really great part about setting and attaining your goals is that once you have reached one goal, you can set another!

You can then begin the process anew, and continue to enjoy your journey!

> *"Arriving at one goal is the starting point to another."* ~ *John Dewey*

> *"Action is the foundational key to all success."* ~ *Pablo Picasso*

> *"Stay focused, go after your dreams and keep moving toward your goals."* ~ *LL Cool J*

> *"What you get by achieving your goals is not as important as what you become by achieving your goals."* ~ *Zig Ziglar*

THOUGHT and ACTION EXERCISE #15

Write down three short-term goals and three long-term goals you want to attain.

List the obstacles you can see yourself encountering. List some possible action steps you can take to overcome these obstacles.

Then list the steps you need to take to reach your goals, and how you will track your progress. (Look at the resources provided and choose one method.)

Short-Term Goals:

1. _____

2. _____

3. _____

Long-Term Goals:

1. _____

2. _____

3. _____

Obstacles

1. _____

2. _____

3. _____

Solutions (ACTION STEPS)

1. _____

2. _____

3. _____

Steps you need to take to reach your goals:

_____

_____

_____

_____

_____

_____

_____

_____

_____

_____

_____

_____

_____

_____

_____

_____

_____

_____

_____

_____

_____

_____

_____

_____

_____

_____

_____

_____

Chapter 16: Assess Your Growth

In Chapter 15, we discussed goal-setting and tracking your goals. This chapter is slightly different. It will explain how you can assess your growth—not your physical growth—your mental growth!

Because your growth is a personal journey, and has no time limits on it, the best way for you to do this is to assess your overall mood each day, and then look back to see how your mood was during prior weeks, to see how far you have come.

If you practice using positive affirmations, as discussed in Chapter 8, your mood will improve drastically within the first month. In fact, you will be able to see changes as early as within the first one to two weeks!

You can use a calendar to help you track how you feel. You can even use smiley faces or faces with frowns on them to indicate your mood. Keeping track of your mood does not have to be a complicated thing!

Here is my rendition of my happy and sad faces:

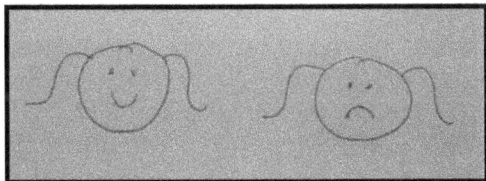

My calendar is filled with more happy faces than sad ones. It's true that I still have some bad days, or days when I feel depressed, because I am human, after all, but it is nice to look at my calendar and see a lot of smiling faces staring up at me! One of my personal goals is to complete a full month using only happy faces!

Another way you can assess your growth is by journaling, which involves writing about your life, the events in it, and what your thoughts are… on a regular basis. You can write each day or each week. Or you can simply write whenever you feel like writing. The key here is to date each entry so you can look back on what you have written and track your growth.

There are many calendar apps and note-taking apps you can install on your phone to do this. There are also daily goal-tracking apps such as iDoneThis to help you, which will send you an email each day as a reminder.

You could also use a paper-lined notebook to write in. You can use your computer and simply create a document to write in. Or you can create a spreadsheet (a table with columns and rows) to use, either on your computer or using paper.

The choice is yours—pick something that is easy for you to do.

For example, you can create something that looks like this:

DATE	OVERALL MOOD	EVENTS OF THE DAY + PERSONAL THOUGHTS
Sunday		
Monday		
Tuesday		
Wednesday		
Thursday		
Friday		
Saturday		

As long as you are able to look back at where you once were and compare it to where you are now, you will be able to tell if you are becoming a happier person.

When you first started reading this book, you were probably filled with sadness and despair. Now that you have learned multiple strategies and techniques for improving your life, altering your beliefs, and becoming a more positive person, I am sure that you feel better.

Through consistent, constant practice and implementation of these techniques, your life is only going to improve! But it is up to you to take action.

The more actions you take, the better your life will become, and the happier you will be!

Just remember, it's okay to fail, too. No one gets things perfect on their first try. The more you do something, the better you will get at it!

> *"It's not about perfect. It's about effort. And when you bring that effort every single day, that's where transformation happens. That's how change occurs." ~ Jillian Michaels*

> *"Do the one thing you think you cannot do. Fail at it. Try again. Do better the second time. The only people who never tumble are those who never mount the high wire. This is your moment. Own it." ~ Oprah Winfrey*

> *"The Universe supports doers." ~ Stephen Richards*

You can also choose to reflect upon your growth in different areas. You can even use the chapters of this book to help you.

For example, you can assess your growth in the following areas:

- releasing negativity from your life (Chapter 7)

- changing your mindset and beliefs through the use of affirmations, meditation, the Law of Attraction, and visualization (Chapters 8 and 9)

- forming healthier habits one step at a time (Chapter 10)

- improving your self-image (Chapter 11)

- using alternative treatments and counselling (Chapter 12)

- spirituality (Chapter 13)

The best way to do these assessments is once a week.

You can also use a numerical rating scale, and watch your number rise as time passes. Or you can simply ask yourself questions and answer with a "yes" or a "no."

For example:

Did I use my affirmations this week?

Did I take the time to meditate this week?

Did I practice the visualization technique this week?

Did I try improving my habits this week?

Did I take steps to improve my self-image this week?

Did I use the EFT tapping method this week?

Did I speak to a counsellor this week?

Did I improve my spirituality this week?

Did I work toward any of my goals this week?

Did I reach any of my short-term goals this week?

Did I make progress on my long-term goals?

By doing a weekly review, you will become more focused on what you really want. As time passes, you will get closer and closer to becoming the person you want to be.

Just remember, big changes take time to make, and going from a suicidal person to a person who is happy and loves life is a HUGE change.

Allow yourself to move forward at your own pace. Do not rush yourself. Do not pressure yourself. Be kind and understanding instead. You'll get there!

If you happen to be a procrastinator, the next chapter will teach you some methods to help you move forward.

THOUGHT and ACTION EXERCISE #16

Which areas of growth do you want to measure?

_____

_____

_____

_____

_____

_____

_____

_____

_____

_____

_____

_____

_____

How will you do this?

Will you make a chart? Will you use a calendar? Will you ask yourself questions?

Write your answers in the space provided.

Once you are done, take some time to create a weekly checklist or table or chart that you can use each week to do this.

You can also use this chart as a template:

DATE	OVERALL MOOD	EVENTS OF THE DAY + PERSONAL THOUGHTS
Sunday		
Monday		
Tuesday		
Wednesday		
Thursday		
Friday		
Saturday		

Chapter 17: Conquer Procrastination

Moving forward is hard. It takes effort and action. Making life changes can be scary! Stepping out of your comfort zone is not always easy!

As a result, many people tend to put things off and tell themselves they will do them later, perhaps when they are feeling better, are more awake, are in the right frame of mind, have more energy, or have more time.

The process of putting something off until *later* is known as procrastination.

Many people procrastinate, and this often causes a plethora of problems for some people. They choose to do something else instead of what they know they should be doing.

They avoid taking action for several reasons. Most of these reasons involve emotions. These people might have a fear of failure, a lack of motivation, a fear of success, and/or a feeling of unpreparedness.

Because they procrastinate, they are not as productive as they should be.

They keep waiting for *the right time* to carry out the task they are putting off.

Has this ever happened to you? I know it's happened to me a million times!

You can be armed with a ton of information (such as the information presented in this book), and *know* what you need to do to move forward, yet, for some reason, you simply don't do anything.

You then get disappointed in or angry at yourself. These negative feelings fester within you, and it is hard to find the energy or willpower to take the steps you need to take to move forward. As a result, you get even more depressed.

It's a vicious, endless cycle.However, it is a cycle that *can* be broken! By learning *why* you are procrastinating and by learning some strategies you can implement to stop procrastinating, you can become a more productive, successful person!

In this chapter, you will learn all these things. Consequently, you will able to conquer your procrastination habits!

> *"Procrastination is the bad habit of putting off until the day after tomorrow what should have been done the day before yesterday." ~ Napoleon Hill*

What does procrastination have to do with eliminating suicidal thoughts?

People who are depressed or are suffering from suicidal thoughts often find themselves in a rut they can't seem to get out of. What's interesting is that they actually procrastinate to protect themselves.

Procrastination is a coping strategy that is hard-wired in our brains. It is a defense mechanism our bodies use to avoid unpleasantness in our lives.

There is a lot of evidence that supports this, too! David Sutton says the following in his e-book, *Procrastination: How to Stop Procrastinating in 10 Days*:

"Procrastination is a coping mechanism to anticipated stress, anxiety, and fatigue… It can also lead to poor emotional and psychological health, as chronic procrastination may lead to *feelings* of inadequacy, guilt, helplessness, self-doubt, and even depression."

Further evidence that procrastination is a psychological defense (also known as a coping mechanism) that we use to avoid unpleasantness in our lives can be found in the online article titled "A Hidden Reason for Suicidal Thoughts."

(http://www.whywesuffer.com/a-hidden-reason-for-suicidal-thoughts/)

Here are two excerpts from that article:

"Suicidal thoughts, as well as acts of suicide, appear to be psychological defenses designed to cover up our unconscious participation in (or emotional attachment to) the experience of inner passivity."

"When people fail to rise effectively to deal with life's challenges, they've likely come under the influence of inner passivity. According to psychoanalysis, inner passivity originates in our psyche's subordinate or unconscious ego… [and is] recognized through its many symptoms, **including procrastination**, fear of intimacy, depression, and weakness in self-regulation."

Another article that supports the notion that procrastination occurs because of an internal fight within your brain is "What Kind of Procrastinator Are You?"

(Found at http://blog.sandglaz.com/5-types-of-procrastinators/)

This article says: "When you are confronted with a task that you don't necessarily like, your limbic system and your prefrontal cortex will fight with each other. Pretty often, it's the limbic system that wins. That's when you decide to leave for tomorrow what you can do today."

To help you better understand this internal struggle and our why procrastination occurs, let's take a look at these two parts of our brain.

The limbic system is responsible for regulating our emotions as well as for our formation of memories and other higher mental functions, such as learning. Our limbic system consists of the following parts of our brain:

- the amygdala (which is the emotion center of our brain)

- the thalamus and the hypothalamus (which are associated with changes in our emotional reactivity)

- the hippocampus (which helps us form memories)

- the cingulate gyrus (which links sights and smells with pleasant memories, induces an emotional reaction to pain, and helps regulate aggressive behavior)

- the basal ganglia (which helps regulate appropriate motor behavior and rule-based habit learning)

The prefrontal cortex is a region in our brains responsible for complex thought processes, expressing our personalities, and moderating our social behaviors. It is also responsible for our decision-making.

Our limbic system deals with our emotions and the way we feel. It is the reason why many activities are pleasurable to us. It is also the reason why it tends to win the fight where procrastination is concerned. We choose to avoid unpleasantness instead of taking positive actions that will help us, because it is just easier to do so!

However, despite our internal struggles, the good news is that procrastination can be overcome... simply by understanding what is going on with our emotional selves, analyzing our present situation, making healthier choices (choices that are going to move us one step closer to attaining our goals) and then taking appropriate action.

We can overcome procrastination by making better choices and taking action.

> *"Procrastination is your body telling you [that] you need to back off a bit and think more about what you are doing." ~ James Altucher*

Procrastination ultimately involves a *choice* between two things.

David Sutton outlines our choices in *Procrastination: How to Stop Procrastinating in 10 Days*:

1. Choosing pleasure over pain, pleasant over unpleasant

2. Choosing easy over difficult, simple over overwhelming

3. Choosing to see a task as an imposition over [an] opportunity

4. Choosing perfection over progress

5. Choosing to escape in the moment over moving forward

6. "Impulse, immediate, short-term" over "deliberate, enduring, long-term"

Perfectionists such as myself are famous procrastinators. That is one reason it took me so long to complete this book—I wanted it to be perfect and this hindered my progress.

With respect to the last chapter on goal-setting, Sutton also agrees with me and many of the things presented in this e-book. He says, "It is convenient to choose urgent tasks that are easy to execute over important goals or tasks that need planning... But you can change your interpretation and action. You can change your mindset, and you can create habits that can minimize procrastination."

So, how can you become more productive and reduce the amount of procrastination in your life? You can use many different strategies and techniques... or "hacks."

5 PRODUCTIVITY HACKS

1: Do something for 5 or 10 minutes each day. By committing yourself to a small interval of time, you are more likely to actually spend that amount of time on your task. However, the premise behind this strategy is that you will want to continue doing whatever it is you are doing once you start doing it.

Remember in Chapter 10 when one of my friends asked me for advice on improving his writing progress, and I told him to write for 10 minutes, starting as soon as he turned on his computer? This strategy worked for him, and he completed a chapter of his book within a week! This technique works!

I used this strategy when I began my weight loss journey. My dietician wanted me to commit to walking at least 10 minutes every day. Initially, I agreed to do this 5 times a week, and made it a habit of doing it in the evening, at 10 o'clock.

After a while, I noticed three things.

First of all, walking became easier the more I did it. When I first started walking, I was severely overweight and worked up a sweat almost instantly. Secondly, the more I walked, the more I wanted to walk! Instead of walking for 10 minutes, I would walk for 20 minutes. Also, the more I walked, the longer it took for me to work up a sweat. Eventually, I worked myself up to 30 minutes, and tried to do walk every day, at the same time each day, regardless of any other physical activity I did.

The third and final thing I noticed was that my body grew accustomed to the routine. As soon as 10 o'clock neared, my body would somehow change and prepare itself for exercise. I cannot explain this change adequately but I can tell you that if I didn't go walking, I felt strange. I felt that way particularly when it was raining outside. I don't like getting wet, and so I would not walk when it was raining. I would then do other exercises from 10-10:30 p.m. because my body was used to moving during that time period!

The only problem I had with walking outdoors arose when winter came. I have a bad leg as a result of an accident I was in. I had two surgeries on it, which saved it but left me scarred for life. Whenever I exert myself, it hurts. It also hurts in cold weather. I noticed my leg would hurt after only 5 minutes of being outside in sub-zero weather.

So, I stopped walking outdoors in the winter and instead found alternate solutions, such as walking in the mall or doing a dance workout to a video or TV exercise program.

Regardless of the issues I faced, the point I am trying to make is that once you start doing something, you will want to keep doing it. You will become accustomed to doing it and will even look forward to doing it each day. As a result, any procrastination issues you had will completely disappear!

2: Another anti-procrastination technique you can use is The Seinfeld Strategy, which involves doing a specific thing related to your goals each day, and marking an X on your calendar each day that you do it, creating a chain.

The goal of this strategy is to continue the chain for as long as you can.

As James Clear says in the online article "How to Stop Procrastinating on Your Goals by Using the Seinfeld Strategy," (found at https://blog.bufferapp.com/stop-procrastinating-seinfeld-strategy):

"The Seinfeld Strategy works because it helps to take the focus off of each individual performance and puts the emphasis on the process instead. It's not about how you feel, how inspired you are, or how brilliant your work is that day. Instead, it's just about 'not breaking the chain.'"

This strategy is one of the 23 anti-procrastination techniques used in Akash Karia's e-book,

This awesome, helpful book is called *Ready, Set...PROCRASTINATE! 23 Techniques to Stop Procrastinating, Get More Done and Achieve Your Biggest Goals.*

If you are a habitual procrastinator, I highly suggest buying and reading this book!

> *"The key to beating procrastination and getting things done is to reduce the pain associated with the task." ~ Akash Karia*

I love Karia's book for three reasons:

1. He provides a summary at the end of each chapter of the key points mentioned in each one.

2. It is extremely informative and easy to understand.

3. He gives you an Actionable Knowledge Application Exercise to do at the end of each chapter.

In fact, I got the idea of providing you with the Thought and Action Exercises from Karia's book!

> *"Never leave till tomorrow that which you can do today." ~ Benjamin Franklin*

> *"Don't wait. The time will never be just right." ~ Napoleon Hill*

> *"You cannot escape the responsibility of tomorrow by evading it today."* ~ Abraham Lincoln

3: Another strategy you can use is the Pomodoro Technique.

This technique is mentioned in Karia's book. It is mentioned in Sutton's book, too, and is something I have known about for a few years.

The Pomodoro Technique was developed by Francesco Cirillo and is a time management technique that allows you increase your work or study habits.

It uses a timer to break down large tasks into smaller ones using short, timed intervals that allow you to have a break after each time interval.

Each time interval is called a "Pomodoro." This is actually the Italian word for "tomato," and is named for the tomato-shaped kitchen timer Cirillo used during his university days, which he used to track his student work!

The technique involves this process:

- Choose a task you want to get done.

- Set your timer for 25 minutes.

- Work until the timer goes off.

- Take a short break.

- Repeat this process.

- After 4 "Pomodoros" (intervals of work), take a longer break.

The reason this technique is so effective is because you get to work or study in short sprints and then take breaks, all which bolster your motivation and productivity.

To time yourself, you can use a kitchen timer, an alarm on your phone, a stopwatch, or a free online timer, such as the Tomato Timer, which is already pre-set to 25 minutes and has the option of using short or long breaks.

The Online Stopwatch Countdown Timer has more options and can be customized easily.

Choose one you like, and use it!

"My advice is to never do tomorrow what you can do today. Procrastination is the thief of time." ~ Charles Dickens

"Life always begins with one step outside of your comfort zone." ~ Shannon L. Alder

"Someday is not a day of the week." ~ Janet Dailey

4: Make a To-Do List and prioritize your tasks. Don't rely on your memory to remember all the tasks you must do or the steps you need to take to reach your goals. Write things down! Then, once you complete an item on your list, cross it off and move onto the next one.

> *"Whatever you want to do, do it now! There are only so many tomorrows." ~ Michael Landon*

To prioritize your tasks, you can use the Eisenhower Matrix, also called the Time Management Matrix.

> *"Success is not obtained overnight. It comes in installments; you get a little bit today, a little bit tomorrow until the whole package is given out. The day you procrastinate, you lose that day's success." ~ Israelmore Ayivor*

This matrix helps you organize and prioritize items on your list of things to do according to their urgency and importance. This matrix is most commonly represented by the following diagram, which Tim Urban from the website Wait But Why calls "The Procrastination Matrix":

(http://waitbutwhy.com/2015/03/procrastination-matrix.html)

The Eisenhower Matrix

	URGENT	NOT URGENT
IMPORTANT	**Q1** DO NOW	**Q2** DECIDE WHEN TO DO IT
NOT IMPORTANT	**Q3** DELEGATE IT AWAY	**Q4** DELETE IT

Other renditions of this matrix have been created too. The following has been used several times on the Internet, in the following posts:

- "Not a morning person? Think again…"

- "Cause 1: The Inability to Organize Details"

- "TIME—tick, tick, tick!"

This diagram clearly shows how to organize and prioritize your tasks.

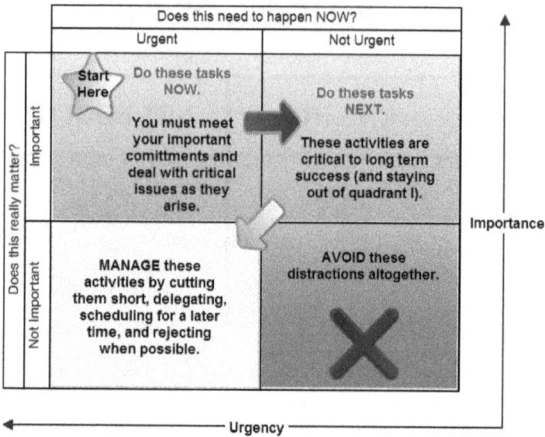

5: Plan your months, weeks, and your days ahead of time, and stick to your plans! Use a monthly planner, a weekly planner, and a daily planner to help keep you on track. Remember to create your plans that reflect your goals (which you created in Chapter 15!)

You can buy or create your own planner, or you can use the free planner offered in my article on Wording Well, titled "How to Find a Good Work-Life Balance (+ a FREE Workbook/Planner)," which also provides further tips on overcoming procrastination and increasing your productivity, all while maintaining a balance in your life.

However you decide to conquer your procrastination is up to you. The key is taking actionable steps, one step at a time!

Remember, life is not always easy. There are going to be challenges along the way. Success does not simply come because you want it. You have to work for it. You have to put in some effort. However, the rewards are great!

> *"You don't have to see the whole staircase, just take the first step."* ~ Martin Luther King, Jr.

As Dr. Richard O'Connor reminds us on the page titled "Procrastination" on his website, Undoing Depression: "Depressed people assume that people who are good at work skills always feel confident and easily attain their goals; because they themselves don't feel this way, they assume that they will never be successful. But again, **most people who are really successful assume that there are going to be hard times, frustrations, and setbacks along the way.** Knowing this in advance, they don't get thrown for a loop and descend into self-blame whenever there's a problem. If we wait until we feel completely prepared and feeling really motivated, we'll spend a lot of our lives waiting."

(http://www.undoingdepression.com/about-depression/quick-tips/procrastination/)

Conquer your procrastination now! Don't wait until tomorrow to do it!

> *"The scariest moment is always just before you start."* ~ Stephen King

> *"Procrastination is the thief of time."* ~ Edward Young

THOUGHT and ACTION EXERCISE #17

In the space provided, answer the following questions:

1. What tasks or chores do you habitually put off until *later*?

2. Which strategies or techniques are you going to try in your efforts to conquer procrastination and eliminate it from your life?

Then take a look at Akash Karia's e-book, *Ready, Set... PROCRASTINATE! 23 Techniques to Stop Procrastinating, Get More Done and Achieve Your Biggest Goals.* I promise it will help you!

_____
_____
_____
_____
_____
_____
_____

FROM NOPE TO HOPE

Chapter 18: How to Make Your Happiness Last

In your quest for learning how to overcome your suicidal thoughts and live a happier life, you have learned many different things!

Let's review your key learnings:

In Chapter 6, you learned some temporary and long-term coping strategies to use.

In Chapter 7, you learned how to identify your emotions and release negativity from your life.

In Chapter 8, you learned how to change your mindset by using positive affirmations.

In Chapter 9, you learned how to use meditation, the Law of Attraction, and the visualization technique.

In Chapter 10, you learned how to form healthy habits one step at a time.

In Chapter 11, you learned how to improve your self-image.

In Chapter 12, you learned of some alternative treatments and were advised to seek counselling.

In Chapter 13, you learned how to increase your acceptance and your spirituality, so you could have more peacefulness in your life.

In Chapter 14, you learned how to create your path to a happier life.

In Chapter 15, you learned how to put your plan into action by setting and attaining goals.

In Chapter 16, you learned how to assess your personal growth.

In Chapter 17, you learned about procrastination and how to conquer it.

Now it is time to apply all you have learned so that you can make your happiness last!

Revisit the different techniques mentioned in this book. Re-do the exercises every few months.

Give yourself permission to be happy, and remember that your happiness depends upon the choices you make.

> *"There is no path to happiness: happiness is the path." ~ Buddha (Siddhartha Gautama)*

Remember to read motivational quotes often and to recite your affirmations every day.

Stay positive and full of hope.

> *"Don't get discouraged. Your time is coming. What you are going through is not permanent. Life is a constant ebb and*

> flow. Sometimes things move at a snail's-pace and then suddenly without warning, change happens in a blink of an eye. So be ready for new possibilities and new beginnings. Truly amazing things can happen in a single moment." ~ Brigitte Nicole

> "You must understand the whole of life, not just one little part of it. That is why you must read, that is why you must look at the skies, that is why you must sing and dance, and write poems and suffer and understand, for all that is life." ~ Jiddu Krishnamurti

Forgive yourself for your past mistakes.

> "If you regret some of the decisions you made in the past, don't be so hard on yourself. At that time, you did your best with the knowledge that you had. At that time, you did your best with the experience you had. If you were to make those decisions with the wisdom you have now, you would choose differently. You would handle life's challenges in more effective ways. So give yourself a break and forgive yourself. Time and experience has a

> wonderful way to make us realize that we prosper, grow and learn to make better choices today, for ourselves and those we care for." ~ Brigitte Nicole

Live life to the fullest, each moment of each day.

> "My mission in life is not merely to survive, but to thrive; and to do so with some passion, some compassion, some humor, and some style." ~ Maya Angelou

Remember that life goes on, no matter what.

> "In three words I can sum up everything I've learned about life: it goes on." ~ Robert Frost

Re-read this book when you get depressed. Keep this book in a special place. Do not file it away somewhere and forget about it.

This book will continue to change your life for months and years to come!

It's changed mine, in many ways! All for the better, too!

THOUGHT and ACTION EXERCISE #18

From reading this book, and doing the exercises, what are the top 3 things that impacted you the most?

Write them down in the space provided. (You can write more than 3 if you want!)

_____

_____

_____

_____

_____

_____

_____

_____

_____

Then email them to me at lorrainemariereguly@gmail.com because I'd really like to hear from you and learn how this book impacted you!

Chapter 19: What to Do If Your Suicidal Thoughts Return

> *"Hope is being able to see that there is light despite all of the darkness."* ~ *Desmond Tutu*

I wouldn't be doing my job as your teacher effectively if I didn't acknowledge the very real possibility that your suicidal thoughts might return.

Regardless of how many changes you make in your life, how many healthy habits you form, or how positive you become, you are going to encounter situations where you will either see, hear, or touch something that is going to trigger bad memories, which will bring you back to a place of darkness and depression.

What you need to do in those situations is to be ultra-aware.

Be aware of what caused your memories, and avoid that trigger, if possible, in the future. Also be aware of your feelings, allow yourself to feel them, and then deal with them in an appropriate manner.

Seek medical treatment. Get yourself assessed. You might have some type of disease or mental disorder that can only be cured through medical treatment and properly prescribed medication.

Also, and I almost hate to say this, but stop being selfish and find a reason to live! Maybe you have sisters or brothers or people in your life who are younger than you, for whom you are a role model. Maybe you have a family member who desperately needs you. Maybe you have a pet who needs you to care for him or her. Think of them and seriously consider how your actions are going to affect them!

Every action has consequences, positive or negative.

Make sure your actions have positive consequences!

Do not be the cause of negativity in someone else's life!

In the next chapter, DK relates his real-life experiences and mentions some of the after-effects of suicide.

I saved his story for the end because of the impact it had on me. I believe it will have the same impact on you, and erase any desire of committing suicide that you might still have.

If or when your suicidal thoughts return, read this book again. Do the exercises again.

Find hope again.

Through it all, know you're not alone!

> *"Hope smiles from the threshold of the year to come, whispering, 'It will be happier.'" ~ Lord Alfred Tennyson*

> *"Optimism is the faith that leads to achievement. Nothing can be done without hope and confidence." ~ Helen Keller*

> *"Our human compassion binds us the one to the other—not in pity or patronizingly, but as human beings who have learnt how to turn our common suffering into hope for the future." ~ Nelson Mandela*

> *"Hope is the magic carpet that transports us from the present moment into the realm of infinite possibilities." ~ H. Jackson Brown, Jr.*

> *"Learn from yesterday, live for today, hope for tomorrow." ~ Albert Einstein*

THOUGHT and ACTION EXERCISE #19

Return to the list of the reasons which you wrote down at the end of Chapter 1 for why you wanted to kill yourself, and write down the solutions for those problems.

For example, if you are in an abusive relationship, how can you go about leaving it or escaping it? Do you need to save money? Do you need to research shelters in your area? Who can you rely on to help you?

_____

_____

_____

_____

_____

_____

_____

_____

_____

_____

_____

_____

_____

_____

_____

_____

_____

Chapter 20: The After-Effects of Suicide: DK's Story

Lots of love, funny quarrels, debates, dreams, and hopes. That was what my family used to have. We were four: my dad, mom, me, and my sister.

Now, we are only three.

One decision changed everything; one aggressive decision when my sister lost hope and turned our lives upside-down.

I have many memories of my sweet sister.

I remember the awesome days when my sister and I used to compete for everything that our dad brought for us.

I remember her stealing my drink, which I drank half.

I remember going to school with her on the bus, holding our hands together. She was two years older than me. She held my hand and made me feel comfortable on the streets.

I remember going with her and my dad to cinemas.

I remember my sister loved using our dad's stomach as her pillow, cuddling up to him. She loved my dad more than anyone on the earth.

I remember when our school days were gone, and college life started for both of us.

I also remember being angry with her.

She married a guy who was her colleague without informing us. None of us knew about her love for him, and was afraid of telling us because she didn't know if our parents would agree to her marriage. When we found out, Mom and Dad were upset, but they loved her a lot, so it didn't take much time to get back in touch with her. At least they felt happy, thinking that their daughter was happy.

I was not opposed to a love marriage but I was angry at her because she didn't inform me about it. We are from India, where many marriages are often arranged marriages or marriages that must be approved by all the parents of the bride and groom.

I changed after her marriage and my behavior towards her also changed. I was rude to her and I didn't talk to her for many months. I stopped caring about her and I ignored her.

But she didn't change.

She still loved me like she did in our childhood. She cared for me, suggested good things to me, and gave me advice to help me develop my career.

When I was dumped by my ex-lover, I cried and stayed in my room for many days.

One day, she came to my room and hugged me. She cried too, and told me that she hated to see me crying. She told me I had to move on with my goals and stop staying in my room.

I really wondered at her love and caring and, frankly, I didn't expect that she would cry by seeing me suffer from my break-up.

A few years after I ignored her, I came to know my mistake. I was wrong and did wrong by ignoring her. She was pure-hearted.

She was married for five years, and was a hard worker. Her willpower was strong.

Whenever she came home, it was like a festival. We were a happy family again.

All of a sudden everything changed... on August 29, 2016.

She passed away, taking all our happiness with her.

What happened:

One day, she called Dad on the phone and told him that she wanted to come home and leave her job. Dad observed that she was upset for some reason and told her to come home, so she did.

She came home and spent her last days with Mom, Dad, and me. We were all were unaware of her thoughts of suicide.

One day, she went to an ice cream parlor and bought her favorite ice cream. Because she was religious, she then went to the Temple. She then mixed some pills into her ice cream and ate it.

She came back home, hugged my mom, and then slept until she started vomiting. She was taken to the hospital where she revealed the truth about her suicide attempt. She was kept under treatment there.

She talked like a roaring lioness as she usually did when she was at home. Everyone thought that she was going to be okay, and asked her the reason for attempting suicide. But she didn't really say.

She died, later that day.

Her kidneys failed as a result of the pills she took.

Whatever the reason might be, what matters now is the suffering and pain she caused us by leaving us.

She was only 28.

At the time of her death, Dad was 52 and hated to see his daughter dying at that age. He stayed indoors for months. He cried most of the time, and felt guilty that he was unable to save his daughter.

He became sick, too, and suffered a stroke in his eye. He now has as a clot now in his left eye, which has reduced his vision.

At night, when Mom and I are asleep, he suddenly starts crying in his bed.

Sleepless nights and hopeless dreams torture my mom and dad mentally.

I tried to be firm and give them hope. But most of the time, I go to my room and cry without them noticing, because if they saw me crying they would feel very low and might get more depressed.

I always try to comfort them, but I fail. Our lives are filled with sadness now.

My sister used to take care of my mother when she suffered from rheumatoid arthritis. She used to take care of my mom whenever she went to the city for treatment. My mom is 50. I am 26.

I saw her crying, saying, "Now I don't have my daughter to take care of me when I go for treatment."

My sister made a claim from her insurance to meet the expenses of my mother's treatment. She did a lot to treat my mother's health condition. But she is no more and now my mom's health is gradually declining.

Now, Dad takes care of her. So do I.

We have a lot of debt now, too, are emotionally drained, and are unable to concentrate on our health.

Frankly speaking, my parents lost their interest in health care. They lost interest in a lot of things.

People can see what's wrong with their health outside but they are unable to see how sick they are mentally.

Every day, they look at pictures of my sister, and touch her clothes and her other things, because they miss her a lot.

Whenever they came across an ice cream parlor they suddenly get upset. My sister liked prawns and whenever they see that dish, they remember her and get depressed again.

Most of the time they don't eat properly. There are no words to mention their suffering.

Or mine.

Though months have passed, we miss her everywhere.

Whenever our relatives celebrate any occasions, my parents skip that. They don't go. Whenever they see a happy family with their daughters, they suddenly change, remembering my sister.

She left us physically, but she is in our hearts. She can't leave us from there.

I don't have anyone now to call with her name, I don't have someone to quarrel with, I don't have someone to share my drinks and food, I don't have someone to guide me like my sister did.

I miss her a lot, as my parents do.

She bought a new shirt for me on my birthday, in May 2016.

I didn't do anything for hers, which was also in May.

She gave me money when I was staying away from my home to look for a job. She took care of me, but I never bothered with her. I even didn't gift her once.

She was elder to me and stood beside me in my success. She drove me to a right path.

She was always there for me, and now I really want to gift her back, but I can't.

I want to tell her that I love her more than I ever showed… but I can't.

I want to have silly fights and quarrels with her, and I want to steal her drink like she did from me when I was a kid… but I can't.

I feel guilty. Lost. Alone. And depressed.

I made a mistake and now I can't correct it. She left me with no choice.

I miss her a lot.

I missed her asking me to bring her favorite food to her. I missed her asking me to go to cinemas with her.

Digesting the truth that a family of four is now a family of three is very difficult.

It's been 9 months since she died and still we are having a hard time.

We always will.

Life is not the same without her.

My plea to you:

I want to say something to those people who are thinking about suicide: Is this what you really want? To have others suffer endlessly because you took your life?

Committing suicide is not escaping from your problems, it is causing more. It's creating a mental suffering to your dear ones and punishing them to live their remaining life missing you in ways you can't imagine.

Please think of my family and our suffering… and use the information Lorraine provides you here to help you change your mind and live a better life.

Please don't make others suffer. Please do not be selfish. Please help yourself.

It is too late for my sister… but not too late for you.

> *"If you want to show me that you really love me, don't say that you would die for me, instead stay alive for me." ~ Unknown*

THOUGHT and ACTION EXERCISE #20

What did DK's story teach you?

What about his story impacted you the most?

_____

_____

_____

_____

_____

_____

_____

_____

_____

_____

_____

_____

_____

_____

_____

_____

_____

_____

Chapter 21: Additional Resources and Available Help

> *"Suicide doesn't end the chances of life getting worse, it eliminates the possibility of it ever getting any better." ~ Unknown*

> *"Suicide is a permanent solution to a temporary problem." ~ Phil Donahue*

There are many online articles you can read for free. There are also many books you can buy to help you.

Plus, there are many hotlines you can call and online agencies you can contact for free, including suicide prevention hotlines and counselling services.

This chapter lists the best ones I have found.

In this chapter:

➢ Articles I Recommend Reading

➢ Books I Recommend Reading

➢ Blogs I Recommend Following

➢ Facebook Pages I Recommend Liking

➢ Additional Resources

➤ Suicide Prevention Hotlines and Counselling Services

Articles I Recommend Reading:

o The Law of Attraction: Where Do I Even Begin?

o The Law of Attraction and How to Master It

o 9 Habits to Manifest Your Dreams Using the Law of Attraction

o Manifest Your Dream Year with This Vision Board Cheat Sheet (This article also provides you with some apps you can use to help you.)

o A Guided Visualization to Help You Overcome Anxiety & Panic Attacks

o The 3 R's of Habit Change: How to Start New Habits That Actually Stick

o How to Change a Habit for Good

o The Habit Change Cheatsheet: 29 Ways to Successfully Ingrain a Behavior

o How to Improve Your Self-Concept and Start Feeling Better About Yourself

o How to Improve Your Self-Esteem: 12 Powerful Tips

- o How to Change Behavior: A Theoretical Overview (This article discusses Dr. BJ Fogg's Behavior Model for changing behaviors, developing new habits, and beating procrastination.)

- o 11 Ways to Beat Procrastination

- o Introducing the Eisenhower Matrix (This article shows how to prioritize tasks based on urgency and importance, thereby allowing you to become more productive.)

- o How to Find a Good Work-Life Balance (+ a FREE Workbook + Planner)

Books I Recommend Reading:

The Courage to Heal Textbook and *The Courage to Heal Workbook* – written by Laura Davis

Ask and the Universe Will Provide: A Straightforward Guide to Manifesting Your Dreams – written by Stephen Richards

Leading You Out of the Darkness into the Light: A Blind Man's Inspirational Guide to Success – written by Maxwell Ivey Jr.

It's Not the Cookie, It's the Bag: An Easy-to-Follow Guide for Weight Loss Success – written by Maxwell Ivey Jr.

Peace in the Present Moment – by Byron Katie

Who Would You Be Without Your Story? – by Byron Katie

Question Your Thinking, Change the World – by Byron Katie

I Need Your Love—Is That True? – by Byron Katie

Loving What Is: Four Questions That Can Change Your Life – by Byron Katie

A Friendly Universe – by Byron Katie

Ready, Set... PROCRASTINATE! 23 Techniques to Stop Procrastinating, Get More Done and Achieve Your Biggest Goals – by Akash Karia

Procrastination: How to Stop Procrastinating in 10 Days – by David Patton

The Power of the Adolescent Brain: Strategies for Teaching Middle and High School Students – by Dr. Thomas Armstrong, Ph.D.

7 Kinds of Smart: Identifying and Developing Your Multiple Intelligences – by Dr. Thomas Armstrong, Ph.D.

The Power of Neurodiversity: Unleashing the Advantages of Your Differently Wired Brain – by Dr. Thomas Armstrong, Ph.D.

The Human Odyssey: Navigating the Twelve Stages of Life – by Dr. Thomas Armstrong, Ph.D.

You Can Win – written by Shiv Khera

Blogs I Recommend Following:

The following blogs/websites are related to positivity, inspiration, motivation, life, and spirituality.

Steven Atchison—Change your thoughts, change your life.

Addicted to Success

Zen Habits

Positivity Blog

Tiny Buddha

Positive Outlook Blog

The Change Blog

Marc and Angel

Live Bold & Bloom

Facebook Pages I Recommend Liking:

Bryant McGill: Author. (Creates beautiful motivational quotes)

Butterfly & Pebbles: Poet. (Creates beautiful quotes)

Awakening People

Ripple Kindness Project (Inspirational stories from school communities and content created by students)

Think Positive Words

My Own Little World

Wings of Encouragement (Helps others with drug and addiction treatments)

Intuitive Guidance with Tracey Smith

Life Mastery by Graham Kean

Di Riseborough—Intuitive Life Strategist

Additional Resources (Internet Articles):

- o Treatment Approaches for Drug Addiction

- o The Key to Stopping Alcohol Addiction Is Personalized Treatment

- o How to Cope with Suicidal Thoughts and Feelings—In Yourself & Others

- o Anger, Depression, and Disability: Adapting to a New Reality

- o The Guide to Rebuilding Bridges with Your Loved Ones after Battling Addiction

- o Earlier Than Too Late: Stopping Stress and Suicide among Emergency Personnel

- o Teens and Peer Suicide: Dangerous Potential After-Effects

- o After a Suicide Attempt: A Guide for Family & Friends

- o Left Behind After Suicide

- o Some Practical Thoughts on Suicide

Suicide Prevention Hotlines and Counselling Services

There are many available resources worldwide that will allow you to call them for free. Simply do an Internet search for "a list of suicide prevention hotlines." You can narrow down your search by adding the name of your city or country at the end. For example, if I were to do a search for available hotlines in my city of Thunder Bay, I would search for "list of suicide prevention hotlines in Thunder Bay."

Various countries, such as Argentina, India, China, America, Mexico, Philippines, Berlin, Africa, Asia, Canada, and the USA provide counselling for preventing suicide. Some of these resources include:

1: AFSP, also widely known as the American Foundation for Suicide Prevention. The

AFSP is an NGO dedicated to curing patients who have suicidal tendencies. They make people aware of curing and maintaining mental health.

2: American Association of Suicidology, also known as AAS. The mission of this foundation is to promote the understanding and prevention of suicide and support those who have been affected by it.

3: Behavioral Health Link, or BHL, which is a 24/7 service provider. They have worked in the field of mental health for many years.

Their professional and caring staff are available anytime (day or night) to help you or a loved one with a mental health crisis or a problem with drugs or alcohol. They can also help you schedule an appointment with a provider.

4: Half of Us, which is a website that is specific to your particular problem. Simply click on the link most appropriate to your problem to get some help.

5: The Jed Foundation, which helps promote emotional health and prevent suicide in young adults.

6: The Link Counselling Center, which is a non-profit community counselling center serving the community since 1971, The Link provides quality, affordable, confidential counselling, psychotherapy, and support groups to all ages.

7: The National Suicide Prevention Lifeline, which is open 24/7. Their number is 1-800-273-8255. No matter what problems you are dealing with, they want to help you find a reason to keep living.

Taken from their website:

"By calling 1-800-273-TALK (8255) you'll be connected to a skilled, trained counselor at a crisis center in your area, anytime 24/7.

When you dial 1-800-273-TALK (8255), you are calling the crisis center in the Lifeline network closest to your location. After you call, you will hear a message saying you have reached the National Suicide Prevention Lifeline. You will hear hold music while your call is being routed. You will be helped by a skilled, trained crisis worker who will listen to your problems and will tell you about mental health services in your area. Your call is confidential and free.

If you feel you are in a crisis, whether or not you are thinking about killing yourself, please call the Lifeline. People have called us for help with substance abuse, economic worries, relationship and family problems, sexual orientation, illness, getting over abuse, depression, mental and physical illness, and even loneliness."

8: The Samaritans, which provide services to people of every age, sex, culture, socioeconomic standing, religion and sexual identity.

They respond to every kind of personal, emotional or health-related problem imaginable, from a bad day or a broken heart to mood disorders and mental illness to a chronic or life-threatening disease, trauma or loss. Their 24-hour crisis hotline number is (212) 673-3000.

The hotline's anonymity and confidentiality also make it a safe point of entry if you are in distress and have not utilized support services in the past or have fears about providing your personal information.

9: The Kid's Help Phone Line (1-800-668-6868), which is a place for teens and children to talk about any topic, including bullying, dating, emotional health, family, LGBTQ, money, jobs, laws, physical health, school, sexting, the Internet, violence, and abuse. Their website also offers live chats with counsellors from Wednesdays to Sundays, from 6 PM to 2 AM EST. If you are 20 years of age or younger, you can use this service.

"The greatest glory in living lies in not never falling, but in rising every time we fall." ~ Nelson Mandela

"Hope is what led a band of colonists to rise up against an empire; what led the greatest of generations to free a continent and heal a nation; what led young women and young men to sit at lunch counters and brave fire hoses and march through Selma and Montgomery for freedom's cause. Hope is what led me here today— with a father from Kenya, a mother from Kansas; and a story that could only happen in the United States of America. Hope is the bedrock of this nation; the belief that our destiny will not be written for us, but by us; by all those men and women who are not content to settle for the world as it is; who have courage to remake the world as it should be." ~ Barack Obama

"When you come to the end of your rope, tie a knot and hang on." ~ Franklin D. Roosevelt

"Most of the important things in the world have been accomplished by people who have kept on trying when there seemed to be no hope at all." ~ Dale Carnegie

"If you want the rainbow, then you've gotta put up with the rain." ~ Dolly Parton

> *"All the great spiritual leaders in history were people of hope. Abraham, Moses, Ruth, Mary, Jesus, Rumi, Gandhi, and Dorothy Day all lived with a promise in their hearts that guided them toward the future without the need to know exactly what it would look like. Let's live with hope." ~ Henri Nouwen*

> *"Hope is my gift to you. Hope for a better tomorrow, hope for a happier life, and hope for being able to live a life worth living." ~ **Lorraine Reguly***

Acknowledgments

From NOPE to HOPE: How I Overcame My Suicidal Thoughts (and How You Can Too) was written to help others overcome their suicidal thoughts and live a happier life.

Many people helped me bring this book into existence.

To my beta readers, who gave me excellent feedback and caught errors in my writing that I missed (it's tough to be the editor of your own work!): Brian Morris, Theodore Nwangene, Tobenna Okoye, Rajan Gohil, David Okedion, Saqib Mamoon, Imran Soudagar, and my brother, Daniel Reguly— Thank you so much for your help! I appreciate your honesty and hope that the final version of this book is one you will be proud of and will share with others.

To my son, Julian Reguly, who encouraged me and hugged me during my tough times— I love you so much! You are the reason I am here and my inspiration to keep on living. I am proud of the man you have become, and I hope you stay proud of me. Your positivity is contagious, your forgiveness is overwhelming, and your strength is incredible. Thank you for all you have done (and continue to do) for me. I am lucky to have such a great son!

To my close friend and colleague, Imran Soudagar—I am fortunate to have you in my life, and I appreciate the time you took to get to know and understand me. Writers often stick together, support one another, and lift each other up during difficult times. Throughout much of the writing of this book, you were my rock. You gave me honest feedback. You took the time to assist me. You helped me in more ways than you could ever know. You were always there for me, and for that I will always be eternally grateful. I can't thank you enough for being the wonderful person that you are! May we continue to help each other as we both move forward in our careers!

To my online friends, fans, and followers— Your continued support and comments on my Facebook status updates (as well as our private conversations) have given me the strength and motivation to finish this book and make it the best it could possibly be. Thank you for not giving up on me… especially when I gave up on myself!

To those who provided me with quotes and testimonials to use (mentioned at the beginning of this book)—Thank you so much for your kind words!

To the three people who contributed their personal experiences—Thank you so much for sharing them and letting others know they are not alone!

To "DK"—I appreciate your contribution so much and truly think your experiences and those of your family will influence others to reconsider their actions when they have suicidal thoughts. The after-effects of suicide are horrendous, and I hope you and your family can find some type of peace someday.

To my deceased Nana Kay (my paternal grandmother)—Although you are no longer physically here, and didn't actually help me with this book, your eternal belief in me "to do something" with my writing abilities has continually spurred me onwards and motivated me to pursue my dreams of becoming a bona fide author. I hope you are looking down on me from Heaven, with love and pride at my accomplishments. I miss you so much and I wish you were still here! Thank you for believing in me.

About the Author

Lorraine Reguly (1971–) was born and raised in Thunder Bay, Ontario, Canada.

By age 4, Lorraine was reading, and by age 6, writing in cursive. She has always had a high IQ, and graduated Grade 8 as valedictorian. High school, however, was more challenging for Lorraine, as she was raped at the age of 14. She was still a virgin at the time, and was completely devastated. She used drugs as a coping mechanism, quit school, and became promiscuous.

After becoming a single mother at age 18, she went back to school and graduated with honours, winning several scholarships and awards.

While Lorraine completed her high school credits, she also sought counselling, finally telling someone about what had happened to her. She became a certified high school Mathematics and English teacher in 1999, and taught for several years. In 2005, she was in an accident in which she nearly lost her right leg.

Throughout her life, Lorraine has had her share of problems. She has done drugs, earned money through prostitution, suffered discrimination as a result of being the single mom of a half-Spanish son, and had suicidal thoughts for years. She attempted suicide once, and has been the victim of depression, too.

A major turning point of her life occurred when Lorraine's appendix burst and she nearly died. She re-connected with her son, and began blogging a few months later, in January 2013. She began a freelance writing and editing business in 2014, and started to take her writing seriously.

Lorraine won the only short story contest she ever entered, and became a contributor to a memoir anthology. She is also a contributing author to a short story anthology.

In 2014, Lorraine self-published her first book of short stories, *Risky Issues*, and has plans for many more books, including an autobiographical memoir series and a collection of letters she wrote to her son. She also plans to write and publish different works of fiction, including a suspense novel and an erotica novella series.

Lorraine blogs at Wording Well (which offers writing, freelancing, and blogging tips to others) and Laying It Out There (where she shares personal stories, book reviews, author interviews, and other things—such as information related to self-publishing. Lorraine also writes poetry, which she shares on that site.

Lorraine loves reading murder mysteries, playing cards, spending time with her family, and shooting pool (playing billiards). She likes cats—even though she's allergic to them—and dislikes snow and cold weather. One day, she hopes to live near a beach so she can go swimming every day when she's not relaxing in a hammock!

The Author's Plea

I would like for you to do these 3 things:

1: Stay strong and full of hope!

2: Tell your friends and family about this book… not just so they might buy it, but to open a dialogue between you and them!

3: Review this book on Amazon for me.

This is important to me. I want to know if this book helped you. I also want others to know about your experience with this book. Thank you!

LORRAINE REGULY

Space for Additional Notes

FROM NOPE TO HOPE

www.ingramcontent.com/pod-product-compliance
Lightning Source LLC
Chambersburg PA
CBHW060003100426
42740CB00010B/1384